MW00736956

AN ARENA FOR EDUCATIONAL IDEOLOGIES

Previous Books

Policy-Making in Education: A Holistic Approach in Response to Global Changes
Teacher Educators as Members of an Evolving Profession
Embracing the Social and the Creative: New Scenarios for Teacher Education

AN ARENA FOR EDUCATIONAL IDEOLOGIES

Current Practices in Teacher Education Programs

Edited by
Miriam Ben-Peretz
Sharon Feiman-Nemser

**Editorial committee: Shlomo Back, Ariela Gidron,
Sarah Shimoni**

The
MOFET Institute
Research, Curriculum and Program Development for
Teacher Educators

ROWMAN & LITTLEFIELD
Lanham • Boulder • New York • London

Published by Rowman & Littlefield
A wholly owned subsidiary of The Rowman & Littlefield Publishing Group, Inc.
4501 Forbes Boulevard, Suite 200, Lanham, Maryland 20706
www.rowman.com

Unit A, Whitacre Mews, 26-34 Stannary Street, London SE11 4AB

Copyright © 2017 by Miriam Ben-Peretz and Sharon Feiman-Nemser
Co-published with the MOFET Institute

All rights reserved. No part of this book may be reproduced in any form or by any electronic or mechanical means, including information storage and retrieval systems, without written permission from the publisher, except by a reviewer who may quote passages in a review.

British Library Cataloguing in Publication Information Available

Library of Congress Cataloging-in-Publication Data

Names: Ben-Peretz, Miriam, editor. | Feiman-Nemser, Sharon, editor.
Title: An arena for educational ideologies : current practices in teacher education programs / edited by Miriam Ben-Peretz, Sharon Feiman-Nemser : with contributions by Shlomo Back, Jacqueline Cossentino, Lella Gandini, Gilad Goldshmidt, Dafna Granit-Dgani, Carolyn Pope Edwards, Raviv Reichert, Esther Yogev.
Description: Lanham, Maryland : Rowman & Littlefield, 2017. | Includes bibliographical references and index.
Identifiers: LCCN 2017000581 (print) | LCCN 2017016034 (ebook) | ISBN 9781475820263 (electronic) | ISBN 9781475820249 (cloth : alk. paper) | ISBN 9781475820256 (pbk. : alk. paper)
Subjects: LCSH: Teachers—Training of—Social aspects. | Teachers—Training of—Cross-cultural studies.
Classification: LCC LB1707 (ebook) | LCC LB1707 .A74 2017 (print) | DDC 371.102—dc23 LC record available at https://lccn.loc.gov/2017000581

∞ ™ The paper used in this publication meets the minimum requirements of American National Standard for Information Sciences Permanence of Paper for Printed Library Materials, ANSI/NISO Z39.48-1992.

Printed in the United States of America

CONTENTS

FOREWORD

IDEOLOGICAL INFLUENCES ON TEACHER EDUCATION PROGRAMS

There has been much discussion about the importance of accountability and teacher quality in teacher education and about how schools and teachers should be updated in order to cope with the demands of changing societies in a globalized world (Lee & Day, 2016). Achieving these goals depends, at least in part, on aligning teacher education with social expectations and with the most effective approaches to teacher education.

But there is no consensus about what societies want from their schools. Nor have we achieved consensus about the most effective ways to prepare teachers. Rather different orientations or paradigms shape teacher education in different contexts and at different historical moments. These orientations may be inspired by local culture, sociohistorical traditions, or "transformative" educational philosophies that are "context-sensitive" (Tuinamuana, 2009, pp. 150–152). As Dror (1992) observes, "Teacher education, as a preparation for teaching in ideological societies, must encompass unique educational principles found in these societies" (p. 45).

Against this backdrop, I am honored to write a foreword for this book that focuses on ideological influences in teacher education. What influences are portrayed here? In many ways the examples in this book embody progressive educational ideologies that emphasize principles of autonomy and democracy. These values or principles are reflected in the kibbutz movement in Israel as well as in schools associated with the Montessori and Waldorf traditions and the distinctive approach of Reggio Emilia. These traditions are associated with innovative, flexible curricula that emphasize individual students' interests and needs (Sliwka, 2008).

This theme comes through in such ideologies as the education in the kibbutz movement in Israel, which for example, promotes child-centered education for "self-actualization" as well as "student and teacher autonomy" (Dror, 1992, pp. 46, 50). Kibbutz education is based on a unity of educational elements, meaning close cooperation between parents, teachers, and informal educational elements within the community. Each age group, a form of autonomous society, is related to an educational group. The group serves as a fundamental pedagogical resource for the education of children as individuals who are part of a group. Thus, the educational process prepares its participants for life in a communal society, the kibbutz.

This book might be viewed as advocating for "alternative education," echoing progressive educational reform. This denotes "different approaches to teaching and learning other than state-provided mainstream education . . . with a special, often innovative curriculum and a flexible programme of study which is based to a large extent on the individual student's interests and needs" (Sliwka, 2008, p. 93).

Montessori schools and Waldorf schools, with their global networks, offer alternatives to mainstream, state-provided education. Maria Montessori's approach aligns well with the thinking of European "progressive" philosophers like Rousseau and Pestalozzi. It advocates a "constructivist" stance with "negotiated" and "emergent" teaching and learning processes (Edwards, 2002, pp. 4, 11). Montessori's educational ideology is grounded in the empirical study of children in learning environments. This child-centered, discovery-oriented focus is guided by clinical observation, experimentation, and refinement of practice. This approach cultivates intimate, long-term relationships between adults and children and among peers. In order to develop and preserve the kind of collective education that was distinctive of kibbutz education, the kibbutz movement established special kibbutz teacher education institutions (Dror, 2002; Kafkafi, 1991; Timor & Cohen, 2013).

The Waldorf philosophy emphasizes the cultivation of children's sensory awareness and their "natural sense of wonder, belief in goodness and love of beauty" (Edwards, 2002, pp. 5, 11). In the Waldorf community, teachers are expected to take continuing professional development in order to develop a deep understanding of the spiritual nature of human beings (Uceda, 2015, p. 143). In keeping with progressive ideologies, Waldorf/Steiner schools also promote children's active, self-directed learning (Sliwka, 2008, p. 99).

The process of becoming a Montessori teacher is related to both theoretical and practical mastery. Becoming a Montessori teacher is not just learning the theoretical basis; it changes the becoming teacher as a person through a complex blend of physical, intellectual, and spiritual activity. The preparation of teacher educators who become the stewards of Montessori theory and practice becomes a central goal in the teacher education process.

Another alternative that has had a significant influence on early childhood education in the United States comes from Italy's Reggio Emilia. This approach is less formalized and emphasizes evolving "experience." It includes distinctive strategies to promote children's intellectual development through a focus on symbolic expression. Such modes of expression might include words, movement, drawing, sculpture, or music. Experiences in such diverse modes of expression lead children to achieve symbolic skills and develop their creativity.

Montessori, Reggio Emilia, and Pistoia share two pedagogical perspectives. They all view education as a "public good," which depends on democratic deliberation among community members, practitioners, and the government on the "meaning of education." Viewing education as a communal activity that depends on the interaction among different community members constitutes a revolutionary pedagogical perspective. Another perspective challenges the "hegemony of the human capital paradigm," which highlights measurable outcomes, standards, and efficiency (Vandenbroeck & Peters, 2014, p. 162) by offering a language of possibility. Once educators focus not only on predetermined measurable outcomes of the education process, they open a horizon of unforeseen possible outcomes that serve individual students, as well as society in general.

The success and proliferation of these alternative education approaches necessitate governmental support. For instance, in Israel, the

Education Ministry has explored full funding for democratic and Waldorf schools (Skop, 2013).

This book makes a valuable contribution to our understanding of the ways in which ideas and values influence teacher education practice. In particular, it examines how different ideologies shape the discourses, content, and pedagogies of teacher education. The book includes cases or illustrations of teacher education in the Montessori, Waldorf, Reggio Emilia, and Pistoia traditions, as well as the democratic tradition embraced by the kibbutz movement in Israel. The diverse teacher education ideologies discussed in this book share an underlying view. Goals, concepts, and practices of teacher education programs are related in their emphasis on the intense connection between teacher education and societal values.

Writing about the importance of ideologies in teacher education, Cochran-Smith (2002) notes:

> Unless underlying ideals, ideologies, and values (about, for example, the purposes of schooling, the knowledge that is most worthwhile for the next generation, and the meaning of a democratic society) are debated along with the "evidence," we will make little progress in understanding the politics of teacher education. (p. 4)

Hopefully, this edited volume will help readers reflect on and explore the ideologies that guide and inform teacher education in their own contexts and beyond.

Understanding the ideological basis of diverse approaches to education might serve educators in their attempt to choose those approaches that are compatible with their educational context. Moreover, examining ideological sources that shape education actions constitutes an additional lens for investigating the realities of the education world.

John Chi-Kin Lee
Chair Professor of Curriculum and Instruction
The Education University of Hong Kong
jcklee@eduhk.hk

REFERENCES

Cochran-Smith, M. (2002). Teacher education, ideology, and Napoleon. *Journal of Teacher Education, 53*(1), 3–5.

Dror, Y. (1992). Teacher education for ideological societies: Taking Oranim, the School of Education of the kibbutz movement, as an example. *Westminster Studies in Education, 15*(1), 45–52.

Dror, Y. (2002). *The history of kibbutz education: Practice into theory.* Tel Aviv, Israel: Hakibbutz Hameuchad (Hebrew).

Edwards, C. P. (2002). Three approaches from Europe: Waldorf, Montessori, and Reggio Emilia. *Early Childhood Research & Practice, 4*(1), 1–16. http://ecrp.uiuc.edu/v4n1/edwards.html

Kafkafi, E. (1991). *A country searching for its people: Termination of the workers' stream of education.* Tel Aviv, Israel: Hakibbutz Hameuchad (Hebrew).

Lee, J. C. K., & Day, C. (Eds.) (2016). *Quality and change in teacher education—Western and Chinese Perspectives.* The Netherlands: Springer.

Skop, Y. (2013, November 10). Education Ministry trying to mainstream democratic, Waldorf Schools. *Haaretz.* Retrieved January 16, 2016, from http://www.haaretz.com/israel-news/.premium-1.558895

Sliwka, A. (2008). The contribution of alternative education. In Centre for Educational Research and Innovation (CERI) (Ed.), *Innovating to learn, learning to innovate* (pp. 93–112). Paris, France: OECD-CERI. http://www.oecd.org/edu/ceri/40805108.pdf ; http://www.oecd.org/edu/ceri/innovatingtolearnlearningtoinnovate.htm

Timor, D., & Cohen, U. (2013). The attitude of the kibbutzim towards the institutions of higher education: From rejection and disagreement to integration. *Iyunim Bitkumat Israel, 23*, 378–410 (Hebrew).

Tuinamuana, K. (2009). Reconstructing dominant paradigms of teacher education: Possibilities for pedagogical transformation in Fiji. In J. Furlong, M. Cochran-Smith, and M. Brennan (Eds.), *Policy and politics in teacher education: International perspectives* (pp. 137–153). New York, NY: Routledge.

Uceda, P. Q. (2015). Waldorf teacher education: Historical origins, its current situation as a higher education training course and the case of Spain. *Encounters in Theory and History of Education, 16*, 129–145.

Vandenbroeck, M., & Peeters, J. (2014). Democratic experimentation in early childhood education. In G. Biesta, M. De Bie, & D. Wildemeersch (Eds.), *Civic learning, democratic citizenship and the public sphere* (pp. 151–165). The Netherlands: Springer.

ACKNOWLEDGMENTS

With feelings of gratitude we thank the people whose assistance was vital for this book.

Special thanks go to Tom Koerner, vice president and editorial director of Rowman & Littlefield, and to Michal Golan, head of the MOFET Institute, for their encouragement, advice, and help. We wish to express our sincere appreciation to John Chi-Kin Lee for writing the foreword to this book.

We thank Yehudit Shteiman, head of Writing Channel and head of MOFET's Publication House; Hanni Shushtari, coordinator of MOFET's Publication House; and Carlie Wall, assistant editor, Rowman & Littlefield, Education Division, for their support and assistance in the preparation of this book.

Special thanks to Tali Aderet-German for her assistance in the editing process of this book.

Many thanks to Anita Tamari for her contribution to the editing process and for her careful proofreading of the text.

We thank Yael Meer for the preparation of the index for this book.

INTRODUCTION

Miriam Ben-Peretz

This volume focuses on the manner in which ideological-societal commitments shape teacher education programs. Through the process of teacher education, ideological movements seek to ensure their impact on society. How do ideological commitments shape the way teacher education programs define what teachers need to know and be able to do? By ideological commitments we mean a system of educational thinking, from which educational frameworks and aims are derived. Ideology might direct the development of education and limit what is acceptable to it. It is a form of pedagogical thinking that leads to educational practices. For example, the commitment to the welfare of students, a pedocentric orientation, might lead to individualized instruction.

The social mission of teacher education might express itself in different perspectives concerning the relation between individuals and the society they live in. For instance, in a society that subordinates the individual to the group, such as the Israeli kibbutz movement, education and teacher education systems embrace practices that enact this ideology, such as involving students in the workload of the members of the collective. On the other hand, societies that value the advancement of the individual, like the United States, tend to develop elaborate systems of testing and evaluation that track the progress of individual students.

In a society that values individual development, teacher education programs might provide courses that foster the teachers' ability to discern and address the needs of individual students. In contrast, viewing students as part of a larger group might call for educating teachers who are skilled at leading group work and who value the products of joint achievement. Such abilities may also require special modes of learning in teacher education, for example, enabling student-teachers to experience the benefits of learning in groups during teacher preparation (Cohen & Lotan, 2014). Bronfenbrenner (1970) made such a distinction in comparing the American and Soviet educational systems. The American system, he argued, puts the individual at the center of educational endeavor, whereas the Soviet system viewed the success of the community as the ultimate goal of the education process.

Adapting a similar distinction might be useful for viewing teacher education processes. As Durkheim (1977) claims in his writing on education and society, educational transformations are always the result and symptoms of social transformations. Durkheim argues that the moral organization of schools must reflect that of civil society outside of school, and that any change taking place in the moral constitution of society will be reflected in the character of education.

An example discussed by Durkheim is that as people's consciousness becomes individualized, education itself must change in order to accommodate new societal assumptions about the role of individual citizens in relation to the state. For Durkheim, this change is reflected in the relationship between the teacher and the student. Individualization and diversification of education are only possible if educators come close to their pupils and get to know their individual nature. Conversely, an education system that views the group as a center of the education situation has to adapt its teacher education programs accordingly. In such a case, teacher education would include knowledge concerning the development of groups, the ways in which their development can be supported, and modes of overcoming difficulties in the ongoing work of groups.

Another important consideration relates to the focus of the education endeavor. In multicultural societies, the education system has to address the needs of minorities, as well as the goals of the dominant culture. This situation raises issues concerning the role of commonalities versus distinctive features of minorities whether ethnic or cultural. How much space should a public education system allocate to learning about minorities alongside the dominant emphasis on the features of the majority? This distinction might relate to a significant number of issues, such as language, religion, history, and family life, as well as norms of individual behavior.

A crucial decision concerns the status of minority languages in the school curriculum—are they part of the compulsory teaching and learning process? Does the history curriculum focus solely on the national history, or does it include the special histories of various minority groups, whether indigenous or immigrants? What holidays are celebrated in school? The national, ethnic, and religious identity of teachers is another sensitive and important issue. What is the potential, as well as concrete impact, of educational ideology on schooling versus the role of political transformations? Different chapters in this book deal with some of these issues.

IDEOLOGICAL INFLUENCES ON TEACHER EDUCATION PROGRAMS

The role of individuals in society versus the focus on communities constitutes one of the guiding factors in planning education in any society. The nature of society, its values, and political and ideological expectations, expresses itself, as well, in programs of teacher education. From this perspective, teacher education serves and promotes desired social agendas, for instance, continuity or change.

Raviv Reichert and Dafna Granit-Dgani, in this volume, present an interesting example of this relationship in their chapter titled "Democracy in Classrooms: The Story of Democratic Teacher Education," which discusses the ideological basis of the democratic schools movement in Israel. The basic assumption is that schools should prepare students for democracy by involving them in democratic modes of decision making. Teachers whose role is to prepare students for democracy require appropriate modes of teacher education. This preparation might express itself in specific courses, for instance, on the nature of democracy.

According to these authors, student-teachers must experience a democratic mode of life in their own teacher education institute in order to understand firsthand what it means to create in their practice a democratic classroom or school. That might mean giving student-teachers a say in curriculum decisions as well as in decisions concerning the teaching staff. Students' decisions should be considered bearing in mind that the criteria used by students, though very important, cannot cover the complexity of teaching. For instance, students might be sensitive to the teacher's ability to relate to them but do not regularly employ criteria concerning the depth of teachers' knowledge.

Similar arguments about the impact of ideology on teacher education are found in the chapter on "Educational Hyper-ideology and the Test of Time" by Esther Yogev. Yogev (chapter 2) elaborates on the relationship between ideology and education in her analysis of the development of teacher education in the Israeli kibbutz movement.

Yogev regards ideologies as systems of beliefs that unify specific groups and guide them in their attempts to fulfill the goals and aims they set for themselves. According to Yogev, the process of development of educational movements might be shaped by excessive engagement with an educational ideology, which she refers to as "hyper-ideology." Noting the short life span of pedagogical hyper-ideology that is characteristic of groups who perceive themselves as avant-garde, Yogev analyzes the rise and fall of certain aspects of teacher education programs in the kibbutz education system.

Another example of how ideology shapes teacher education is captured in Cossentino's chapter on Montessori teacher education. This chapter, "Montessori and Practice in Teacher Education," examines how ideology informs the practice of Montessori education and the practice and discourse of Montessori teacher education. The major assumption of this chapter is that Montessori practices are grounded in a "cosmological" worldview reflected in the interactions of teachers and students. Cossentino states that "within the Montessori worldview, healthy human development is directly linked to an optimistic vision of social reform fueled by compassion, respect for nature, and commitment to realizing human potential" (see chapter 3 in this volume). These commitments are reflected in what Montessori teachers need to learn and how Montessori teacher education programs help them learn that.

Sometimes distinctive ideological approaches to teacher education develop within local educational frameworks. Such is the case of the innovative early childhood programs in northern and central Italy, which Lella Gandini and Carolyn Pope Edwards discuss in their chapter, "What Can Teacher Educators Learn from Italian Preschools?" Gandini and Edwards explain how innovative early childhood programs in Reggio Emilia and Pistoia, Italy, generated new processes of teacher preparation and ongoing development. The authors detail the elements of strong early childhood education and explain how that vision is translated into teacher education and teacher development in Reggio Emilia and Pistoia.

Gilad Goldshmidt, in his chapter, "Integrating Waldorf Education Principles with Traditional Teacher Education," writes about the relationships and challenges of combining principles of Waldorf education with academic studies and teacher preparation. His chapter shows how the ideological-spiritual studies of Rudolf Steiner influenced the curricula and teaching methods in Waldorf schools and in Waldorf teacher education programs. Steiner's views of children and educational processes are expressed in a holistic, multifaceted approach to teaching and learning. This is evident in Waldorf schools, which strive to balance the theoretical, artistic, and physical domains in the teaching schedule. The aim is that by the end of schooling, each child experiences all these fields of learning, among them art and aesthetics.

Shaping education and teacher education processes according to certain ideologies might narrow their scope. The stronger the impact of ideology on the content and the processes of an educational endeavor, the more it might limit and diminish the professional integrity of education programs. Shlomo Back discusses the dark side of the power of ideological influence in education. In his chapter titled "Undermining Teacher Education: Neoliberal Worldviews," Back analyzes neoliberal worldviews and their impact on teacher education and warns against adaptation of neoliberal teacher education programs.

Domination of education by ideology or any belief system is one of the risks of educational planning. Focusing on one aspect of planning, for instance, learners' potential interest in a given area of study, might lead to neglecting other important components of education. The educational planning process has to consider the complexity of knowledge and modes of learning.

Writing about the relationship between ideology and teacher education reforms, Cochran-Smith (2002) claims that the question of how to prepare high-quality teachers cannot be resolved by relying solely on empirical evidence regarding teachers' actions in schools, but must also debate the various ideological and political aspects on which reform agendas are based. "Once the ideological basis of social practice is acknowledged, then it stands to reason that debates about how to reform practice—including educational practice—need to address openly the difficult choices and trade-offs that all choices about values and ideology entail" (p. 3). Ideology and values are central components of political transformations in any society. Such transformations have far-reaching consequences for education and teacher education.

REFERENCES

Bronfenbrenner, U. (1970). Reaction to social pressure from adults versus peers among Soviet day school and boarding school pupils in the perspective of an American sample. *Journal of Personality and Social Psychology, 15*(3), 179.

Cochran-Smith, M. (2002). Teacher Education, Ideology, and Napoleon.(Editorial). *Journal of Teacher Education*, 53(1), 3.

Cohen, E. G., & Lotan, R. A. (2014). *Designing groupwork: Strategies for the heterogeneous classroom* (3rd ed.). New York, NY: Teachers College Press.

Durkheim, E. (1977). On education and society. In J. Karabel & A. H. Halsey (Eds.), *Power and Ideology in Education* (pp. 92–105). New York: Oxford University Press.

I

DEMOCRACY IN CLASSROOMS

The Story of Democratic Teacher Education

Raviv Reichert and Dafna Granit-Dgani

Democracy faces great opportunities and great risks. On the one hand, the freedoms of individuals and communities that previously suffered from oppression are becoming stronger, and on the other, the institutions that underpinned classic and modern democracy are being undermined (Eisenstadt, 2005). We seem to be called up to respond to Dewey (1916), who argued that the role of education in a democratic country is to develop democratic consciousness in educators and students, and transform the founding principles of democracy into a tangible part of educational reality.

Indeed, there is a revival in the adoption of democratic pedagogy in educational fields. This revival is also evident in recent decades in teacher education in various places around the world, among them Finland (Jyrhama et al., 2008) and the United States (Darling-Hammond & Bransford, 2005). In recent years, teacher education programs founded on democratic pedagogy have been developed in Israel as well (Greinfeld & Bar Lev, 2013).

This chapter presents the story of Shvilim, a teacher education program in the spirit of democracy. The program was established in 2012 and is the product of a collaboration between the Institute for Democratic Education and Kaye Academic College of Education. The objective of the Institute for Democratic Education is to bring about social change by advancing a culture of democracy with a focus on the educational and academic world as a springboard for change;[1] Kaye Academic College of Education is a long-standing teacher education college in Israel's southern region and a leader and innovator in the field.

LIBERTY, EQUALITY, AND FRATERNITY: THE PRINCIPLES OF DEMOCRACY AND THEIR EXPRESSION IN DEMOCRATIC PEDAGOGY

What is democratic pedagogy? What is the connection between pedagogy, which is the theory and practice of education, and democracy, which is a system of government?

We have chosen to open the discussion on the essence of democratic pedagogy with statements made by two central figures in the history of democracy. Abraham Lincoln stated that democracy is the "government of the people, by the people, for the people," and Immanuel Kant, the great philosopher of the Enlightenment, during which modern democracy was formulated, wrote, "Man can only become man by education."

Lincoln's statement is part of the Gettysburg Address, which he delivered during the American Civil War, at the dedication of the Soldiers' National Cemetery in Gettysburg, Pennsylvania, four and a half months after the Battle of Gettysburg, which was a turning point in the war, in order to lift the spirits of his audience and instill in them a sense of partnership in creating an American identity.

Kant's statement indicates that education is intended to develop and shape all that is naturally inherent in man, and which is hindered to him since he is in a state of minority, which prevents him from knowing the world and making his way in it (Weinryb, 1995).

Lincoln's statement raises numerous questions, such as: Who are "the people"? How can "the people" govern? For whose benefit does government act? And Kant's argument contains the answers to these questions: it is education that constructs a person who is capable of leading and/or participating in a "government of the people," which is the basis of democracy.

In his *Democracy and Education*, Dewey (1916) clarified the connection between democracy and education. According to him:

A society which makes provision for participation in its good of all its members on equal terms and which secures flexible readjustment of its institutions through interaction of the different forms of associated life is in so far democratic. . . . Such a society must have a type of education which gives individuals a personal interest in social relationships and control, and the habits of mind which secure social changes without introducing disorder. (p. 86)

Thus Dewey (1960) introduced the concept of "participatory democracy," which has been prevalent in the discourse on democracy since the 1960s. This concept holds that every effort must be made to bring citizens closer to government in order to enable them to make decisions. By means of their active participation in government, citizens will fulfill democracy, which should be a way of life in which they can shape their destiny (Hermann, 1995). Dewey viewed education as a means to making the vision of participatory democracy a reality.

The principles of the democratic vision are stated in the motto of the French Revolution, which constitutes the definitive political expression of democracy to this day: Liberty, Equality, Fraternity.

Democratic governments can be characterized by these three principles and the dialectics between them. Throughout the history of democracy, liberty, equality, and fraternity have been the cornerstones of the democratic discourse, and they gain expression in each of its definitions, from the earliest definition of "government of the people" to the contemporary postmodern definition that speaks of a democracy of cultural pluralism that accords legitimacy to the self-governance of a society's subcultures.

The essence of democratic pedagogy is transformation of the definitive principles of democracy into educational reality, and development of a democratic consciousness in learners who experience this reality. Democratic pedagogy discusses three fundamental issues: What is learning? Who is the learner? and Who is the educator? through a dialogue with the three principles of democracy: liberty, equality, and fraternity.

What Is Learning? Learning Based on Liberty

The conservative, technical-rational approach, aspires to educate from the top down in accordance with values dictated by a central system.

This approach resembles cognitive taming and/or training that emphasizes conditioning, reinforcement, and informed imitation (Back, 2012).

In contrast, the democratic approach gives learners a voice and emphasizes their experience, not only during their education but throughout life. This kind of learning experience can only exist under conditions of liberty.

These conditions mean eliminating coercion in education, and providing choice and its attendant responsibility as a firm foundation of the educational process (Dewey, 1916). Accordingly, learning is meant to take place by constantly questioning the authority of knowledge and the learning processes themselves. Questioning enables learners to create their own knowledge from the ocean of existing knowledge and find the learning methods suited to them.

In *Democratic Education: A Beginning of a Story*, Yaacov Hecht (2005), the founder of democratic education in Israel, argues that learning is in fact a dialectic journey between not knowing and knowing, a journey attended by constant growth and development. The search for knowledge and the constant questioning concerning its validity compel the learner to embark on a constant quest for more updated knowledge, which in turn raises new questions.

Hecht contends that this is not a Sisyphean journey, but the only journey that enables learning and development. In the course of this journey the learner's knowledge and character are constantly being renewed. The driving force of this journey, according to Hecht, and following Goleman's emotional intelligence theory (1998), is the potent emotional experience stemming from the process of discovery and the attendant sense of growth. It is not the cognitive element that constitutes the basis for the motivation to learn, but rather the strong emotional element of learning that transforms it from a burden into an experience.

Who Is the Learner? The Learner Who Has the Right to Equality

Paulo Freire coined the metaphor of the learner as a "piggy bank," an empty vessel to be filled with knowledge by educators, whereby success in learning is measured by the degree to which the vessel is filled. A teacher who successfully fills the learner's head with knowledge is a better teacher. A "vessel" that obediently agrees to be filled, thus relinquishing his right to decide what he does or does not wish to contain, attests to a better student (Freire, 1970, p. 1).

The democratic education approach holds a different view: learners have a natural right to fully and completely develop their character, and the right to be equal to every other learner. These rights can only be fulfilled in a dialogical setting that constantly allows learners to choose the learning content they desire from an appropriate variety of possibilities. The variety of choice is created in a dialogical process between learners and teachers, the latter striving toward maximal attentiveness to the learner, all the while presenting their outlooks within the dialogue.

Learners also have the right to choose the learning method. Because learners have varied learning intelligences, unique needs, and an individual rate of learning, their right to choose should be expanded and fulfilled as well. This combination of choosing learning contents and methods enables learners to discover their strengths, namely, the learning abilities they possess and have not yet identified, or perceived, and to continue developing them.

This combination allows learners to get to know their "areas of growth," the places they will reach out of curiosity or intuition, and discover that they are meaningful to help them grow. Encounters will be more exciting and stimulating, and will provide learners with the mental fortitude required for learning. It is the dialogical setting that enables equality, fulfillment of the equal right of all learners to learn, with their diverse strengths, areas of growth, and fields of interest (Hecht, 2005).

Fulfilling the learner's right to learn will result in meaningful and productive learning and personal empowerment. Furthermore, it will enhance the development of a tolerant and active human being who respects the other and his rights, and is prepared to act for their fulfillment.

Who Is the Educator? Educating through Fraternity

The essential role of the democratic teacher, or "facilitator of learning" (Rogers, 1969), is to create a community of learners founded on fraternity, with facilitators who will allow the learners to formulate the community's language, its culture of discourse and listening, and its unique procedures.

A worthy community exists in conditions of constant dialogue and choice, and these conditions enable it to formulate its rules and determine the discussion procedures within it, as well as ways of handling conflict. For the community to provide true support for its members, the teacher must create an atmosphere that encourages acceptance, trust, discussion, learning, and "being together." The more the community acts, experiments, and critically examines the processes taking place within it, the better it will be able to strike roots and ensure the fulfillment of its mission (Cunningham, Bennett, & Dawes, 2000; Rogers, 1969).

Consequently, in democratic education, the teachers are very different from the authoritarian, all-knowing teacher. They strive to work together with their students by listening to them and displaying empathy toward them, by enabling meaningful learning, and helping them to realize their humanity. Together with the learners, the teachers will seek the profound meaning of their joint endeavor, fulfilling Buber's demand for a dialogical relationship in which "if the word comes to us and the answer proceeds from us then human life exists . . . in the world" (Buber, 1980, p. 255).

Educational Configurations Expressing Democratic Pedagogy

There are numerous educational configurations that express democratic pedagogy, from the Socratic discourse, which was formulated in the fifth century BCE and expresses the spirit of Athenian democracy, to place-based education, which is currently being formulated and expresses the spirit of activism in contemporary democracy. We shall now present two highly influential educational configurations that are relevant to the Shvilim Program, and that clearly express democratic pedagogy.

The first configuration is the different versions of the open democratic school, from Summerhill School, which was established by Alexander Sutherland Neill in the early twentieth century, to the democratic schools in the late twentieth and early twenty-first centuries.

These schools provide a learning experience through liberty, equality, and fraternity. They are governed by a democratic system that in its essence expresses these three principles, and include a legislative body that affords learning through participation in a community discussion of the school's rules, a judiciary body that affords learning through conflict resolution, and an executive body that affords learning through doing for the benefit of the school community.

The formal learning in these schools is based on the learner's choice from a range of diverse contents and learning methods. The different learning settings in which lessons, workshops, task groups, and so forth may be held are created from the learners' choices, and enable the creation of a community of learners based on fraternity out of free choice. In these schools each learner is usually accompanied by a personal mentor of his or her choice. The mentor accompanies the learner in constructing the learning processes by means of meaningful dialogue. Thus the learner experiences liberty and fraternity (Reichert, 2012).

The second pedagogic configuration is schools in which the primary form of learning is project-based learning (PBL). In PBL, doing is at the heart of the learning process. Mounting an exhibition, building an instrument or structure, writing a play, going out to demonstrate, teaching a lesson, holding a public debate, or editing a film can all drive a learning process.

PBL is a learning method whereby students freely initiate a methodical inquiry process that focuses on a complex and authentic question or problem, and develop the project under the teacher's guidance. The project provides a place for their "voice," freedom, and choice, and they demonstrate in-depth knowledge of academic content and learning skills that express fraternity and dialogue. This kind of learning is directed toward teamwork, brainstorming, communicating with peers and experts, and generally concludes with a presentation before an audience.

This approach can be seen as a product of the philosophy and endeavor of John Dewey and his pupil and successor William Heard Kilpatrick. PBL has an extensive history of educational experimentation—for example, about one-quarter of schools in the United States in the 1920s and 1930s implemented these methods, as did hundreds of schools in Israel's kibbutz education system and labor educational approach schools.

However, this teaching/learning approach was unable to contend with the demand for scholastic achievements and standardization, and demanded extensive time and investment from the teachers, and subsequently disappeared with the crises of the twentieth century, which resulted in a return to traditional learning methods.

There has been a revival of PBL principles since the early 1990s, and even more so in the early twenty-first century, which have been accorded new meaning. One of the clear expressions of this revival is the High Tech High network of schools in San Diego, California, in which PBL is implemented. The learning is interdisciplinary as are the projects, many of which invite activism and consequently a combination of liberty, equality, and fraternity (Ram, 2011).

THE IMPORTANCE OF DEMOCRATIC EDUCATION IN OUR TIME

The role of democratic education, to transform the founding principles of democracy into an educational reality, becomes even more significant in our time, at a time of great opportunities for democracy alongside risks.

These opportunities and risks stem from the extensive changes associated with cultural and economic globalization, and from the ideological and institutional developments in a postmodern, multicultural direction. The global changes strive to increase liberty and equality in society. Previous, relatively rigid definitions of modes of living, of family, community, sociospatial organization, and of occupational, gendered, and territorial roles have all loosened and weakened in recent decades, and are likely to frequently reassemble into new configurations.

These trends have developed new nuclei of cultural and social identity that transcend existing cultural and political boundaries, resulting in far-reaching changes in the institutional foundations of existing democracies.

Among these changes are the formation of direct relationships between political publics and different political players, and the rise of the media in real and online environments, and its importance in the political process. At the same time, these processes are likely to lead to the erosion or weakening of the fundamental components of democratic regimes, such as rule of law, or the penetration of nondemocratic fundamentalist elements that are gaining strength and are liable to change the spirit of the basic society (Eisenstadt, 2005).

TEACHER EDUCATION THAT PROMOTES A CULTURE OF DEMOCRACY

We are now witnessing the beginning of an imminent historic change in teacher education. Extensive bodies of research and reference attest to the conservatism of teacher education through the generations. Ducharme and Ducharme (1998), who wrote about the history of teacher education in the United States, claim that the training programs are remarkably consistent and continue to preserve the authoritarian patterns established in colleges that were founded in the Unites States in the early nineteenth century. Levin and Horin (2004) found that most teacher educators in Israel have traditional educational outlooks.

The conservatism of teacher education is consistent with the conservatism of academe in general. Despite great historic transformation, such as the French Revolution and the upheaval of the 1960s, the customary pedagogy of lectures, demonstrations, memorizing, and imitating has remained largely unchanged.

Listening to a lecture delivered by a scholar has been the accepted method of learning since the establishment of the first universities in the Middle Ages. Research became part of university studies after the scientific revolution permeated the universities in 1810 when von Humboldt established the first research university in Berlin (Rudy, 1984; Schechter, 2006).

Conservatism is also addressed in Schechter's *Cracks in the Ivory Tower*, which states that even with the most innovative means it is not easy to overturn a didactic tradition of hundreds and perhaps even thousands of years of university teaching (Schechter, 2006). This conservatism created a clear distinction between academe and the general education system, which has experienced numerous revolutions in the two hundred years since it was first established in Prussia, France, and Austria (Ram & Hecht, 2008; Reichert, 1998).

The general education systems were more attentive to social changes and accorded them greater space than academe. This gap between the education system and the academic world prevented teacher education from fulfilling one of its purposes—to connect the two worlds. In other words, the general education systems made room for democratic education, whereas teacher education programs, which were meant to train teachers for an education system in a democratic country, suffered from the conservatism of academe, and thus failed to provide appropriate teacher education programs.

The influence and presence of democratic pedagogy have become increasingly evident in the general education systems. Among the reasons for this presence is the democratization of knowledge that attended the information and communication technology revolution.

Other reasons are the increasing importance of initiative and creativity in the contemporary labor market, the children's rights revolution, the loss of absolute truths in postmodern reality, and increased multiculturalism in the population (Ram & Hecht, 2008). This increase is also associated with the crisis experienced in academe in the past two decades as a result of the globalization of knowledge, greater possibilities for higher education at home, and the privatization of research (Schechter, 2006).

The rise of democratic education in the general education systems has been accompanied by a rise in democratic teacher education. In the United States, the number of democratic teacher education institutions and programs has grown considerably since they were first established in the 1990s, and this has affected educational endeavors worldwide.

The teacher education programs at Bank Street College of Education, Antioch College, and Sarah Lawrence College are examples of democratic pedagogy in education. Many other such programs, whose influence extends beyond the schools in which their graduates teach, can be listed, among them the Secondary School Teacher Education Program at John Carroll University, the Education for Civic Responsibility Program at Ohio University, and the Accountability Leadership Institute at the University of California (Cappel, 1999; Novak, 1994).

Preparing Teachers for a Changing World, a report published in 2005 by the National Academy of Education Committee on Teacher Education, formulated the basic perceptions concerning teacher education.

The writers of the report claim that the aim of education is to prepare all students for equal participation in a democratic society, equal access to the resources and opportunities society offers, and for equal participation in civic, political, and economic life. Consequently, teacher education should equip novice teachers with the tools to provide a democratic experience in the classroom and at the school, to encourage learning based on diverse intelligences, for evaluation and not only measurement, to manage communities of learners and not only discipline them (Darling-Hammond & Bransford, 2005).

A revival in the implementation of democratic pedagogies is evident in Israel Ministry of Education documents and programs as well. *Yisrael Ola Kita* (Israel goes to the next grade) is a Ministry of Education (2013) document that includes democratic pedagogy as a central component of the core curriculum in schools. Another document published by the Ministry of Education (2014), *Academia—Kita* (Academe—Classroom) is a plan to form a connection between teaching experience and democratic pedagogy.

There are currently four democratic teacher education programs in Israel. The Experimental Open Education Program at David Yellin Academic College of Education, the first of its kind in Israel, was founded in the 1970s by Moshe Caspi. Since the beginning of the twenty-first century three additional democratic teacher education programs have been established:

The Martin Buber Beit Midrash for Dialogue Education at Beit Berl Academic College was founded by the Dror Israel youth movement in conjunction with the college in 2000; at about the same time, the Incubator for Educational and Social Initiatives was established at Kibbutzim College of Education, and these were joined in 2012 by the Shvilim Program at Kaye Academic College of Education. The two latter programs were established by the Institute for Democratic Education in conjunction with the host colleges.

The following is a description of the Shvilim Program, which was established as a dedicated democratic teacher education program.

THE SHVILIM PROGRAM: DEMOCRATIC TEACHER EDUCATION

The Shvilim Program was established through a collaboration between the Institute for Democratic Education and Kaye Academic College of

Education in Beer Sheva. In 2012–2013 the program was recognized as an experimental program by the Division of Experiments and Initiatives at the Israel Ministry of Education, and is still in operation at the time of this writing in 2016.

Shvilim is a four-year training program that grants its students a B.Ed. in social-environmental education, a teaching diploma in geography, and an education worker certificate, with emphasis on working with youth at risk or youth and community. Two disciplines are taught in the program, geography and nonformal education, constituting twenty-six credit points each, as well as education studies and experience in democratic education, which constitute thirty-seven credit points.

A team of representatives from the Institute for Democratic Education and the college was chosen to develop and build the program. The team consists of nine lecturers, who also serve as "incubator mentors" who mentor a small group of students. In the year 2017, 207 students are learning in the "shvilim" program: first year: 60 students; second year: 55 students; third year: 55 students; fourth year: 37 students. In the first class that graduated last year were 22 students. At total count there are 229 students in the program until now.

Shvilim Student Characteristics

Students applying to the Shvilim Program undergo an admission interview and are accepted on the basis of their educational experience. They complete a personal information questionnaire in which they present their educational vision in brief, and answer questions on their perception of the educator in the twenty-first century, addressing political, environmental, and social questions and dilemmas. After passing the admission interview, candidates are required to meet accepted academic admission conditions, such as matriculation and psychometric exam scores.

The program was designed to suit mature students with educational experience who can and should continue working in education during their studies. From their first to their final year of study the students are awarded credit points for their practical workplace experience, thus maintaining a close connection with the educational field, as opposed to the disconnection that often occurs in teacher education programs.

The students bring extensive knowledge from their educational experience when conducting case studies or presenting examples from their teaching field, and find connections between theories learned in the program and the field. We, the coauthors of this chapter, serve as pedagogic instructors in the program, guiding the students along the didactic paths and accompanying them in their practical experience in the schools. Thus, we frequently witness the fascinating connections created throughout the program between the theories presented in the didactic workshops and the students' educational backgrounds. Due to the students' educational experience, especially in nonformal frameworks, a rich dialogue is created in the course of the sessions.

The Characteristics of Learning in the Shvilim Program

Democratic pedagogy, the axis of the program, is manifested in three dimensions: constructing knowledge on democracy and democratic pedagogy, acquiring democratic teaching skills, and participating in the creation of a democratic experience. Through the combination of these three dimensions the Shvilim Program seeks to create a synergetic democratic environment.

The Knowledge Dimension: Developing Knowledge about Democracy and Democratic Education

In this dimension, the aim of the program is to expand the students' knowledge about democracy and democratic education. The program includes courses designed to deepen the students' knowledge of the content worlds of democracy and democratic education.

These courses address questions such as "What is democracy?," "Why is there a need to train teachers for a culture of democracy?," and "What are the connections and disparities between a democratic environment and a school environment?"

The program includes courses such as Democratic Educational Thought, in which the students are introduced to various thinkers in the field of democratic education; Democratic Education Configurations, which includes educational tours of democratic and progressive schools all over the country; and Educating for Democratic Values, in which students gain in-depth understanding of the central values of democracy and their fulfillment (or nonfulfillment) in contexts of active citizenship, state institutions, political-economic contexts, and so forth.

Another aspect of the program that contributes to deepening the students' knowledge and understanding of democracy is the connection between the different disciplines studied—geography and environment, nonformal education and democratic education. As stated by Glassner (2014), "The sense of discovering new, different, unexpected connections that are not self-evident, and wandering between associations and especially connotations, lead to enhancement and broader meaning" (p. 2).

The grouping of disciplines into combined courses in the program develops a broad worldview, and gives the students the means to examine the various strata and contexts of social phenomena. The artificial separation in standard teacher education programs, which is consistent with the perception of the studied subjects in schools (first lesson—physics; second lesson—civics; third lesson—English) limits thinking. Conversely, addressing a particular issue from diverse angles and from different disciplines and theories enables in-depth observation and development of critical thinking.

Thus, the course People in the Desert, which belongs to geography studies, is grouped with Children and Youth Leadership in the Negev for one concentrated study week. In this grouping between the two courses the distinctiveness of children and youth leadership in the Negev region in Israel's south is examined. It engages with questions such as how the unique location influences and is influenced by the interaction between Israel's geographical center and periphery, and how the term "distributive justice," which has political implications within the democratic outlook, is manifested.

Other examples of grouped courses in concentrated study weeks include Adult-Child Dialogue in the sphere of educating for democracy, which is paired with Empowering Youth at Risk in the sphere of nonformal education; and Community of Learners as a pedagogic method and Open Spaces or Disadvantaged Spaces as a geography issue in the field of environmental quality.

The Skills Dimension: Acquisition of Democratic Teaching Skills

Alongside theoretical knowledge, the aim of the program is to develop teaching and evaluation skills in future teachers. In democratic education these skills are based on the principles of choice, learning from experience, and conducting meaningful dialogue as part of the democratic experience, about which we shall expand in the following section. Based on the value of liberty and an understanding that true learning stems from processes of questioning, searching for and locating a solution for gaps and misunderstandings, and contending with choice, the Shvilim Program provides learners with possibilities to assume personal responsibility for their learning processes.

The students are invited to choose their courses and lecturers, the study days suited to them, the special emphases recorded on their certificates at the conclusion of the process (e.g., in-depth study of "youth at risk" or "youth and community"), learning methods, and task groups, all of which comprise their democratic experience. In most courses the students choose how they will be evaluated and how they can most successfully express their learning process. In their first and fourth years the students choose the place for their practical experience.

Many of the courses are based on PBL, a method that expresses the values of democratic pedagogy and grants the students extensive freedom to deconstruct and rebuild a broad subject of their choice, and create diverse learning products in accordance with their strengths. These courses provide opportunities for group learning and the numerous challenges and advantages this entails. For the most part, the students choose which task group they belong to.

Examples of broad subjects learned in the program in which PBL skills are employed include Center and Margins and Political Education—Life in Israel Following Operation Protective Edge (the 2014 military operation in the Gaza Strip). PBL enhances the sense of meaningful learning by granting learners relatively extensive freedom concerning what they learn and how they learn. The program emphasizes projects that can contribute to one community or another.

A worthy project is directed toward contending with generative topics; investigating authentic issues; developing creative thinking; teamwork; employing collection, classification, and processing skills; and presenting knowledge (Glassner, 2014).

The principle of experiential learning (Kolb & Kolb, 2005; Schneider, 2006) is very prominent in the program. Many of the courses utilize personal experience to develop the learners' reflective ability to conceptualize their actions after the fact, and draw conclusions from their active participation, rather than from reading an article or position paper on the subject. Employing discretion, interpretation, and creating and attributing a value are all part of any meaningful learning (Aloni, 2014).

Ecological Space is an example of an experience-based course, where the students build an educational ecological garden in the college. Another is Journey: Individual—Group—Desert, in which the students go on a three-day journey in the desert equipped only with what they can carry and without any means of communication. In Outdoor Training (ODT)—Walking the Beer Sheva Trail, the students experience ODT learning methods by learning about the region of the city of Beer Sheva.

Most of the courses in the program draw on place-based learning, encountering the students with the field, encouraging awareness of the place in its broad meaning, and assuming responsibility that invites activism in a local context. This educational configuration expresses fraternity between individuals and between the individual and the place.

In accordance with a general directive from the head of the program, the lecturers are expected to incorporate at least one educational tour per course. If such a tour is not possible, lecturers can invite people from the educational field to the lesson in the form of a panel of experts (e.g., police personnel) or guest lectures, or conduct a cooking therapy workshop or a theater workshop.

Most of the cultural-human geography courses include visits to locations in the Negev region and meetings with influential figures or people with unique and interesting stories. Emphasis is placed on direct encounters with much of Israel's southern region, the Negev Desert, where the college is located.

One of the central skills practiced in the program is conducting meaningful dialogue, which, essentially, expresses fraternity. These are dialogues between one and oneself, and between one and one's identity, between mentor and mentee, between lecturer and student, between student peers, between the student and the community of learners in the program, and between the student and the physical and human environment in and outside the college on local and global levels alike.

For a dialogue to be meaningful for us it must connect with personal identity and self-determination and influence personal narrative. Meaningful dialogue according to Aloni (2014) is a situation wherein students see their teachers as people who genuinely care about them, are interested in the students, and want the best for them. Together they can progress into new realms of understanding, enrichment, inspiration, and creativity.

Meaningful dialogue in democratic education endeavors to enable the individual to move in the world of knowledge and find his or her distinctive path. The principle of conducting a multifaceted, meaningful dialogue is particularly prominent in the following course in the program:

The Incubator—From Personal Empowerment to Social Activism is a four-year course (eight credits). The course promotes the understanding that areas of learning influence our personal, educational, and scholastic objectives and are influenced by them. Each student in the course belongs to an "incubator"—a small (up to thirteen members) study group. The course is based on Cunningham's (Cunningham et al., 2000) self-managed learning (SML) model, which proposes a process for developing independent learning skills by engaging in five central questions: Where have I been?, Where am I now?, Where do I want to get to?, How will I get there?, and How will I know if I have arrived?

In their first year the students undergo a self-search process from the past to the present. In the second year, the process focuses on deepening and specializing in a field of knowledge that interests the learner. In the third year, "production" takes place in which every student experiences actual creation in the social, educational, personal, or environmental world.

A production can take the form of developing a curriculum on a particular subject, creating collaborations, establishing a voluntary association to contend with a specific social need, writing a book of poetry, or mounting an exhibition of pictures describing the process the student has undergone throughout his or her journey of discovery. In the fourth year the students are asked to disseminate the product of their production in the relevant educational field.

The products are varied and diverse, but the learning orientation from the inside out, from finding personal distinction to social influence, is the axis along which the course moves. For the individual, the group serves as a hall of mirrors, a reference group, an arena and incubator for personal development process. Personal and group dialogue feature prominently in the incubator. The incubator-mentor conducts personal monthly meetings with each student, aiming to provide attention and listening, and to make time for in-depth processing of experiences in the group meetings.

The nine Shvilim staff members conduct frequent meaningful dialogue on the program's management. Dilemmas, experiences, new ideas, and suggestions for developing and improving the program are raised and discussed in regular, weekly meetings. We have had the privilege of being pioneers and creating the program "with our own hands," thinking together with great flexibility, adapting to the students' needs, and ensuring relevance.

At times the students ask to join the staff meetings and raise subjects for discussion. In discussions with students who participated in the staff meetings we discovered that these meetings constitute a model for them, parts of which can be adopted for teamwork and joint leadership of creation and development processes. The synergy created in these meetings facilitates productive and flexible division of the educational, administrative, and pedagogic burden.

The Democratic Experience Dimension: Creating a Democratic Experience

In addition to knowledge and skills, the community of learners, which is based on the values of fraternity and equality, provides students with an experience of participating in a culture of democracy. To do so, the structure of political democracy and the administration of open democratic schools has been borrowed, and the program has legislative, executive, and judiciary bodies.

In the legislative body, the Parliament, there are seven students and one staff member. The Parliament discusses topics and issues from the program's life, and also examines ideas and values, such as the value of transparency between the committees, the issue of representation of the various years in the committees, establishing new committees in accordance with changes in the program's needs (e.g., a graduates' committee or a work placement committee).

The executive body consists of committees established to advance various matters in the program, with three to seven students on each committee and one staff member. A variety of committees were elected and are currently active, among them a lesson schedule committee, a cultural activity committee, a newspaper committee, a learning environment committee, course committees (accompanying and developing content and evaluation methods together with the course lecturer), a study day committee, and an activism committee.

The judiciary body operates in the form of an ethics committee that discusses important everyday issues for the proper operation of the program. These may include tardiness, absenteeism, and failure to meet academic requirements.

Although joining a committee is voluntary, there is a very high attendance rate in each of the committees, and for the most part third- and fourth-year students lead the committees alongside a member of the teaching staff. Participation in the committees facilitates frequent learning of the system and gaining a deeper understanding of the processes taking place in the program. It also develops independence, involvement, cooperation, and initiative on the part of committee members.

Each committee is supported by a member of the teaching staff. It provides an opportunity for a different kind of acquaintance between lecturers and students, which is not based on academic work. Staff members and students work as equal partners to carry out social-scholastic tasks, such as producing a study day or cultural event for the Jewish and Arab (Muslim and Christian) festivals and holidays, publishing a newspaper, and so forth.

Once a semester, the students attend a Community Day. The day includes Parliament sessions as well as events we call Open Spaces. The Open Spaces are intended for short peer learning workshops on subjects of student specialization and/or toward which they can contribute (e.g., a student specializing in dance may lead a short dance session for everyone).

Many students attest that participating in Parliament sessions and Community Days has shaped their attitude toward the program. This participation has transformed the program from a means to obtaining an academic degree to a journey of belonging to a group that inspires a desire to influence and take an active part in the Shvilim community.

The synergy between the program's three dimensions—knowledge, skills, and experience grounded in the values of democracy—creates an educational reality that develops democratic consciousness and a culture of democracy. This is learning from experiencing democracy in practice by contending with conflicts and issues typifying a democratic environment (Eisenstadt, 2002).

Conflicts are an important part of the dynamic of the Shvilim Program, and democracy cannot be experienced without putting them on the table and learning from the way we manage them.

Conflicts and Dilemmas that Emerged in the Program

Democracy facilitates a society that possesses great inner strength that frequently changes and is built as a result of inherent conflicts (Eisenstadt, 2002). Alongside the desire and aspiration to operate a democratic program and provide a democratic experience, we have also encountered challenging dilemmas and conflict situations that this kind of program invites.

The basic contract signed between a student registering for the program and the program's leaders from the Institute for Democratic Education and the college speaks of a four-year training program at the conclusion of which the student is awarded a B.Ed. On occasion there is a contradiction between the need to meet the program's academic requirements and maintaining a democratic environment and spirit. Some of the compulsory courses do not enable fulfillment of the principle of choice, such as Hebrew language, Judaism, and research methods.

Furthermore, a significant proportion of courses necessitate a numerical grade, whereas the democratic environment is directed toward a more qualitative and participative evaluation. In order to create a uniform language common to all the lecturers in the program, the program's leaders hold a plenary meeting with all the lecturers once a semester. In this meeting they discuss generic topics such as evaluation methods and dealing with the diverse populations and cultures in the program.

One such case, in which a contradiction emerged between the democratic principles of freedom of expression and freedom of choice and the need to meet academic requirements in order to receive a degree was extreme: on a Community Day during which a Parliament session was held with all the members of the program, a group of students requested that an ethics committee be established in order to formulate and implement rules of ethics in the program.

Once established, a committee discussion revealed that some of its members viewed the committee as a tool to remove students from the program. This engendered a debate that raised the typical democratic conflict between minority rights and majority rule. Representatives of the program staff in the committee highlighted the problematic nature of the intention to remove students from the program by their peers, which resulted in the group of students leaving the committee. The committee was subsequently reestablished with another group of students whose intentions regarding the ethics committee were different. As leaders of the program we felt we had touched the boundaries of democracy and its dangers with caution and resolve.

Another complex case occurred during Operation Protective Edge, in the summer of 2014. In a student forum that is also active on Facebook, offensive posts were exchanged between right-wing and left-wing students. A harsh dispute ensued between the students that peaked with an appeal to the staff to bridge and mediate between the adversaries. To address the situation, we enlisted students from both sides of the political divide. Each group presented its positions concerning Operation Protective Edge and its effects on the schisms between Jews and Arabs, and between supporters of the political Right and Left.

The debate turned out to be fascinating and moving. It included confessions concerning feelings of fear, guilt, danger, and the need to survive, bringing tears to the eyes of some of the participants. Most of the participants left the meeting amazed by the intensity of the arguments from both sides, and there was a sense of constructive and liberating dialogue. For us, the staff, it constituted a positive and defining example for conducting a complex dialogue between extremes from which the students were able to learn how to deal openly yet sensitively with difficult dilemmas in a culture of democracy.

In Way of a Summary

In this chapter we have sought to examine connections between a democratic society and its values and democratic pedagogy and its fulfillment in the unique Shvilim teacher education program. We have shown how the fundamental values of democracy—liberty, equality, and fraternity—serve as the foundations for building three teacher training dimensions in the program—knowledge, skills, and a democratic experience. Finally, we presented conflicts and dilemmas from the program's everyday life.

In our estimation, the secret of the Shvilim Program's success to date lies in its flexible and open growth, which also includes the emergence of complex dilemmas, missteps, and mistakes, all of which are perceived as a springboard for improvement and change.

Central to the program is a constant examination of the fulfillment of the values underlying it in the everyday practices within it. In our view, this is the heart and core of democratic pedagogy in the Shvilim Program.

NOTE

1. www.democratic.co.il

REFERENCES

Aloni, N. (2014). Constructing meaningful experiences in education and learning: Guidelines for educators and teachers. *Journal of the Institute for Progressive Education, UNESCO Chair for Humanistic Education*. Tel Aviv, Israel: Kibbutzim College of Education (Hebrew).

Back, S. (2012). *Ways of learning to teach: A philosophically inspired analysis of teacher education programs*. Rotterdam, Netherlands: Sense.

Buber, M. (1980). *I and thou (Besod Siach)* (Z. Woyslawski, Trans.). Jerusalem: Bialik Institute (Hebrew).

Cappel, C. (1999). *Utopian colleges*. New York, NY: American University Studies, Series 14, Education, Vol. 38.

Cunningham, I., Bennett, B., & Dawes, G. (Eds.) (2000). *Self-managed learning in action: Putting SML into practice*. Aldershot, England: Gower.

Darling-Hammond, L., & Bransford, J. (Eds.). (2005). *Preparing teachers for a changing world: What teachers should learn and be able to do*. San Francisco, CA: Wiley.

Dewey, J. (1916). *Democracy and education: An introduction to the philosophy of education*. New York, NY: Macmillan.

Dewey, J. (1960). *The child and the curriculum: The school and society*, (C. Braver, Trans.). Tel Aviv, Israel: Otzar Hamoreh (Hebrew).

Ducharme, E. R., & Ducharme, M. K. (1998). *The American Association of Colleges for Teacher Education: A history*. Washington, DC: American Association of Colleges for Teacher Education.

Eisenstadt, S. N. (2002). *Democracy and its tortuosity: Paradoxes in modern democracy*. Tel Aviv, Israel: Ministry of Defense Publications (Hebrew).

Eisenstadt, S. N. (2005). *Paradoxes of democracy: Fragility, continuity, and change* (R. Bar Ilan, Trans. & Ed.). Baltimore, MD: Johns Hopkins University Press.

Freire, P. (1970). *Pedagogy of the oppressed*. New York, NY: Herder and Herder.

Glassner, A. (2014). Teaching that increases the likelihood of experiencing a sense of meaningful learning. *MOFET Institute Journal, 52* (Hebrew).

Goleman, D. (1998). *Working with emotional intelligence*. New York, NY: Bantam Books.

Greinfeld, N., & Bar Lev, B. (2013). Department of Teacher Education: From theory to practice. In S. Shimoni & O. Avidav-Unger (Eds.), *On the continuum: Training, induction, and teachers' professional development—policy, theory, and practice* (pp. 27–59). Tel Aviv, Israel: MOFET Institute and Ministry of Education (Hebrew).

Hecht, Y. (2005). *Democratic education: A beginning of a story*. Jerusalem: Keter and the Institute for Democratic Education (Hebrew).

Hermann, T. (1995). *From bottom to top: Social movements and political protest, 1*. Tel Aviv, Israel: Open University (Hebrew).

Jyrhama, R., Kynaslahti, H., Krokfors, L., Byman, R., Maaranen, K., Toom, A., & Kansanen, P. (2008). The appreciation and realisation of research-based teacher education: Finnish students' experiences of teacher education. *European Journal of Teacher Education, 31*(1), 1–16.

Kolb, A. Y., & Kolb, D. A. (2005). Learning styles and learning spaces: Enhancing experiential learning in higher education. *Academy of Management Learning & Education, 4*(2), 193–212.

Levin, Tamar & Horin, Ariel. (2004). Affinities between educational views and epistemological beliefs among teacher educators. http://portal.macam.ac.il/ArticlePage.aspx?id=385.

Ministry of Education. (2013). *Yisrael Ola Kita* [Israel goes to the next grade] (Hebrew).

Ministry of Education. (2014). *Academia—Kita* [Academe—Classroom] (Hebrew).

Novak, J. M. (1994). *Democratic teacher education programs, processes, problems, and prospects*. Albany, NY: SUNY Press.

Ram, E. (2011). A PBL learning community: The pedagogy for the third wave. *Kriat Benayim, Journal for Junior High Science and Technology Teachers*, 22–33 (Hebrew).

Ram, E., & Hecht, Y. (2008). Dialogue in democratic education: From individual empowerment to social activism. In N. Aloni (Ed.), *Empowering dialogues in humanistic education*. Tel Aviv, Israel: Hakibbutz Hameuchad (Hebrew).

Reichert, R. (1998). The idea of democratic education and the platform of Western thought. *Siman She'ela, 8–9*, 34–39 (Hebrew).

Reichert, R. (2012). Why do we create configurations of democratic pedagogy? *Democratic Pedagogy: A Roadmap*. Institute for Democratic Education, 105–115 (Hebrew).

Rogers, C. (1969). *Freedom to learn: A view of what education might become*. Columbus, OH: Merrill.

Rudy, W. (1984). *The universities of Europe, 1100–1914: A history*. Lanham, MD: Fairleigh Dickinson University Press.

Schechter, S. (2006). *Cracks in the ivory tower*. Tel Aviv, Israel: Tzivonim (Hebrew).

Schneider, K. (2006). A century of democracy and education: Reflections on the work of John Dewey. In G. Arnsberg, P. Fenn, & K. Schneider (Eds.), *Democracy—education—society: Aspects of their interrelationship in Israel and Germany*. Freiburg im Breisgau, Germany: Fillibach-Verl.

Weinryb, E. (1995). *An interpretation of Kant's "Prolegomena."* Tel Aviv, Israel: Open University (Hebrew).

2

EDUCATIONAL HYPER-IDEOLOGY AND THE TEST OF TIME

Esther Yogev

Ideology underlies all decisions in the field of education. When we say that education operates by virtue of ideological legitimacy, we mean that ideology is a system of consciousness from which educational orientations and aims are derived.

At its initial emergence, a new educational ideology imbues its proponents with a sense of completeness and excitement, and facilitates the creative structuring of groundbreaking pedagogical thinking, educational practices, and everyday behaviors. Later, those who espouse the ideology in question may be unable to accommodate its demands, and adaptations are made to the pedagogical positions that guided the original ideology.

Based on the premise that ideology underlies all educational discussion, we will turn to examine the historical story of two teacher education institutions established by the Israeli kibbutz movement in the mid-twentieth century. Both institutions presented themselves as a distinct hyper-ideological alternative to the hegemonic system of education at the time.

At its initial emergence, this alternative approach sought to integrate the principles of progressive education with the goals of socialist Zionism and the construction of kibbutz as a complete way of life. However, historical analysis of the kibbutz movement's approach to teacher education, from its initial emergence up to the present day, reveals a protracted, shifting struggle that began with an effort to preserve its unique

character and concluded in 2015 with the quiet surrender of its pedagogical independence.

KIBBUTZ "COLLECTIVE EDUCATION" AS HYPER-IDEOLOGY

Kibbutzim were founded as an original and innovative creation of the
labor Zionist movement in Palestine at the beginning of the first decade
of the twentieth century. For the young European Jewish immigrants to
pre-state Palestine who built and inhabited them, as well as many others, the kibbutz symbolized the possibility of establishing and maintaining a voluntary egalitarian society based on direct democracy and the
fundamental complementary components of communalism and a pioneering, Zionist, task-focused orientation.

From the start, education was a cornerstone of the kibbutz ideology.
This chapter will explore the changes that have occurred in the formative ideology of kibbutz collective education by tracing the development
of the kibbutz movement's approach to teacher education. The changes
that took place in the two teacher education institutions from their
establishment up to the present will provide explanatory insight into the
functioning and life expectancy of alternative pedagogical ideology.
These changes will also be viewed in the wide context of Israeli society
and the entire kibbutz movement.

Pedagogical ideologies can be conceived of as acting concurrently in
two opposing ways: as a problematic force with reductive and limiting
potential, and as a positive force with the potential to empower and
inspire (Guess, 2001; Yuval, 2015). The mid-twentieth-century theoreti-
cians who spearheaded the denunciation of ideologies in the spirit of
ideas advanced by sociologist Daniel Bell (*The End of Ideology*) argued
that all ideologies are, by nature, closed, dogmatic, and inflexible, despite the shimmering fantasies they purport to represent (Bell, 1960;
Gouldner, 1976; Shils, 1968). The ideas were subsequently bolstered by
postmodernist thinkers, who maintained that ideologies are always
teleological, totalitarian systems with metaphysical foundations (Bartes,
1972; Foucault, 2002; Lyotard, 1999).

Conversely, the positive view regards ideologies as systems of beliefs
that unify specific groups and guide them in their attempts to fulfill the

goals and aims they set for themselves. Political philosopher Martin Seliger defined ideology as a force that motivates positive action in the practical and creative sense of the word. In addition to this positivist definition, Seliger noted the empowering combination between the factual substance of specific ideologies and the moral commitment of those who embrace them (Seliger, 1976).

Historical processes that are revolutionary in nature reflect the central role assumed by pedagogical ideology, which becomes *hyper-ideology* when it inundates and takes control of most elements of life. At the heart of hyper-ideology lies the natural human impulse to seek out grand meaning, based on the assumption that a coherent, comprehensive conception can provide solutions to the fundamental questions facing the group and that a corresponding system of pedagogical strategies can ensure its application in practice. Pedagogical hyper-ideology, a characteristic of small groups who perceive themselves as avant-garde, guides all aspects of their lives.

However, a key problem of pedagogical hyper-ideology is its relatively short life span. This short life span is a result of the fact that alongside the human impulse to seek out grand meaning there is always an opposing impulse—the impulse for normalcy and the promotion of our own personal welfare, and that of those close to us, through undisturbed daily life. The complexity of the social experience of everyday life, explains cultural scholar Terry Eagleton, causes the different components of hyper-ideology to collide with one another in a manner that requires it to engage in interminable negotiation regarding its identity. In this way, the ideological system itself always encompasses processes of compromise and adjustment, between the total worldview on which it is based, on the one hand, and its more operative components on the other hand (Eagleton, 1991).

Education scholar Miriam Ben-Peretz (2008) proposes using "lifecycle" as a metaphor describing the development, implementation, decline, and reemergence of pedagogical innovations. These innovations, which usually develop during times of comprehensive economic and political change, present fundamental, ideological challenges to the field of education. Ben-Peretz distinguished between the life cycle of individual reform endeavors and the cyclical reemergence of the same reform, noting that the fate of a specific reform is influenced and shaped by power relations and "parallelograms of forces" among different constituencies (Ben-Peretz, 2008, p. 11).

The pedagogical concept of hyper-ideology and the life cycle metaphor offer useful insight into the changes that have occurred in kibbutz teacher education over time. These changes will be traced from the initial establishment of kibbutz education as a prominent pedagogical alternative, through its theoretical atrophy in the 1980s and 1990s, to the emergence of the revival program (the second wave) toward the end of the 1990s. As we will see below, this dynamic of revival has had a different impact in each of the kibbutz movement colleges.

Educational historian Yuval Dror (2002) has noted the major identifying features of kibbutz collective education:

1. The kibbutz regarded itself as responsible for educating its children within a learning environment based on the fostering of a close, everyday relationship with the kibbutz community and its life experiences. Until the mid-1980s, most kibbutz children lived, slept, and studied in kibbutz children's houses (*batei yeladim*), spending only a few hours a day with their parents in the parents' homes.

2. One key principle of the kibbutz education system was its "unity of educational elements," which took the form of close cooperation between parents, teachers, and nonformal youth educators.

3. Each age group was seen as an "educational group," and regarded as a fundamental pedagogical resource for the individual and social education of the child, from infancy through adulthood. Through processes of guided independence, kibbutz education nurtured the autonomy and self-sufficiency of communities of kibbutz children and youth ("children's societies" and "youth societies").

4. In the spirit of progressive education, the kibbutz embraced a holistic ecological educational approach that encompassed experiential and multidisciplinary process learning, daily encounters with the nearby natural environment and community life, and manual labor.

5. The educational staff of the kibbutz education system worked autonomously (not under the supervision of the Ministry of Edu-

cation), planning and developing their unique curricula and running the overall pedagogical program.

The effort to preserve the unique distinction and even elitism of kibbutz collective education was manifested in the establishment of kibbutz teacher education institutions (Dror, 2002; Kafkafi, 1991; Timor & Cohen, 2013). The doctrine of "collective education" as a pedagogical ideology made its way from kibbutzim to the teachers' education schools as life experience and returned to them as a comprehensive concept, complete with a unique and creative system of practices.

In its early days, the hyper-ideology of kibbutz teacher education fulfilled the needs of kibbutz founders for grand meaning, providing them with values, a collective historical narrative, and a future pedagogical vision, and imbuing them with creative energy and a sense of completeness. Later, far-reaching changes occurred in the nature of the kibbutz life and in the kibbutz's formative position in Israeli society, and influential processes of privatization and economic and political change depleted its financial strength (culminating in the complete financial collapse of numerous kibbutzim). Many young adults left their kibbutzim, and the need to survive yielded changes and adaptations in kibbutz life in general and kibbutz education systems in particular.

Since the late 1930s, the kibbutz teachers' education schools have been facing issues connected with the uniqueness of their professional training. Indeed, the initial aims of kibbutz teacher education have changed, and the programs are aligned with the state teacher education curriculum. Nonetheless, the ideological message and the unique practices that gave birth to kibbutz education appear to be deeply rooted and resurface time and again in the pedagogical field in different formats. This ongoing ideological revival offers a living example of a fascinating pedagogical life cycle.

In this chapter we will look at the two teacher education schools established by the kibbutz movement—the Kibbutzim College of Education (Seminar Hakibbutzim), and Oranim Academic College of Education, and apply a comparative historical analysis of their development. In doing so, we will explore the duality of kibbutz pedagogical hyper-ideology in its encounter with the constraints of its changing context, and highlight the protracted, shifting struggle to preserve its unique character. The sources consulted for this study were gleaned from the archives of the two schools and the kibbutz movement archives at Givat Haviva and Yad Tabenkin.

The comparative analysis considers three phases in the evolution of these institutions: (1) 1930s–1970s: establishment, joining the state education system in 1950s and 1960s, and the beginning of academization in the 1970s; (2) 1980s–1990s: professionalization; and (3) 2000–2015: second education wave—ideological revival to the official break from the kibbutz movement.

1930s–1970s: KIBBUTZ TEACHER EDUCATION FROM ESTABLISHMENT TO ACADEMIZATION

Seminar Hakibbutzim was established in Tel Aviv by Palestine's three kibbutz movements in 1939, and a northern branch, Oranim, was added in 1951. Oranim was intentionally situated in a rural location, in contrast to the urban location of Seminar Hakibbutzim. In 1951, the same year, the broad political schism that split the kibbutz movement also split the school, resulting in the establishment of a separate institution at Beit Berl. Initially known as the College for Collective Education, Beit Berl operated until 1963 as a third arm of the kibbutz movement. Approximately ten years later, the kibbutz movement abandoned its branch at Beit Berl due to poor student recruitment and transferred it to the Moshavim Movement[1] (Hever Hakvutzot, 1951).

From the outset, then, the establishment of the kibbutz teachers' education schools bore marks of both unity and division. The first director of these institutions, Mordechai Segal, believed in fashioning a teacher education program in the spirit of both socialist Zionism and the tradition of American progressive education.

Segal maintained that such a program would suit the kibbutz way of life and differ fundamentally from the standard secular approach to teacher education being conducted in the country at the time.[2] Segal was strongly influenced by John Dewey, as well as by Jean-Jacques Rousseau, Robert Owen, Sigmund Freud, Janusz Korczak, Maria Montessori, and, later, Siegfried Bernfeld and Gustav Wyneken. He joined forces with Shmuel Golan, who developed the psychoanalysis-influenced psychological-pedagogical approach to "collective education" (Golan, 1961), and natural science educator Yehoshua Margolin (Margolin, 1957; Segal, 1972), who would later establish a botanical garden, a petting zoo, and rich zoological collections for the study of the natural sciences at Oranim. In the early years of the three kibbutz teachers' seminaries, the subject matter was socialist in nature and consistent with the humanist spirit of kibbutz ideology; even biology was taught from a Marxist perspective. Lysenkoism was taught at length, and biblical criticism was the prevalent approach to Bible studies (Segal, 1992).

From their establishment and until the 1970s, Seminar Hakibbutzim and Oranim developed teacher education that was creative, original, multifaceted, and influential. Their approach included experiential and investigative process learning outside the classroom—the "process method," developed by Mordechai Segal in the spirit of Dewey's ideas (Kafkafi, 1998). It also included the interdisciplinary study of integrative subjects (the "subject method"), psychoanalytic conceptualization of the educational field (Golan, 1961),[3] and the pedagogical construction of "collective education" as an all-encompassing doctrine.

During the first two decades of Israeli statehood, both schools were run in accordance with the communal spirit of kibbutz life, pedagogically and organizationally. The students lived on campus, went home only once every two or three weeks, were integrated into the planning of the curriculum, and were full partners in running the institutions' everyday life (Segal, 1956, 1992; Yogev, 2011).

Contending with the Anti-academics Ethos

From their very inception, the kibbutz teacher education schools faced a crisis of identity. The kibbutz movement's founding generation sought to remove the exilic Jewish scholarly tradition from the character of the new Jew, living a productive life in the Land of Israel, and instead to glorify the uneducated worker. Meir Ya'ari, a leader of the Kibbutz Artzi, Hashomer Hatzair's settlement movement, expressed his oppositional views regarding academics and higher education as follows:

> The shomer [Hebrew for "guard," a term often used by Hashomer Hatzair and Kibbutz Artzi to refer to devoted movement members] in the land of the Hebrews does not daydream. For dozens of generations, our ancestors have dreamed more than enough. We must place our emphasis on educating a generation of activists . . . not

pens, paper, and ink; not odes and anthems; not confessions and the spilling of the soul; but rather saws, axes, hoes, and, first and foremost—hands! Give us your hands! (Ya'ari, 1947, p. 11)

At the moment the kibbutz movement decided to demonize the academy, an equation emerged between Diaspora mentality and excessive spirituality. For this reason, a necessary precondition for the success of kibbutz as a way of life was the emasculation of the revolutionary's intellectual dimension in an effort to be an "earthy" person of work and manual labor.

In the 1950s and 1960s, during which Israel's higher education system underwent dramatic growth, this uncompromising approach to academic study caused many kibbutz members to abandon their kibbutzim (Timor & Cohen, 2013). Between 1955 and 1959, thousands of kibbutz members left their kibbutzim, and the following decade, the number of members who left their kibbutzim outnumbered new arrivals by 9,100 (Pavin, 2007).

This anti-academic ethos also had a critical influence on the perception of the role of the teacher on a kibbutz. Teachers frequently experienced a sense of inferiority vis-à-vis kibbutz members with more visibly manual jobs. The fact that teachers were not perceived as "productive" was detrimental to their public status. In an effort to contend with the anti-academic ethos, the kibbutz movement related to the work of kibbutz teachers not as an academic profession but rather as a public mission. Segal describes the unique character of kibbutz movement teacher education at the seminaries as fundamentally contrary to that engaged in by the universities:

> It is neither alienating vulgarity nor a shop for higher education. There is no distance between the teacher and the student, no judging people according to their grade alone, and no withered scholarliness in an academic corner. The seminary in its entirety must be a learning community, pushed forward by a shared assemblage of ideas, aspirations, and experiences that together constitute a bridge to the designated, appointed role of this community, according to whose will it was established. (Segal, 1956, p. 261)

In 1953, the Israeli parliament (Knesset) enacted the Compulsory State Education Law, and in so doing made the decision to do away with most of the independent educational "streams" that had operated during the pre-state period. Termination of the "workers stream" officially placed the kibbutz teacher education schools under the authority of the Israeli Ministry of Education. The kibbutz movement could no longer maintain its own private training system, as it now required official government authorization and budgetary support. Within just a few years, Seminar Hakibbutzim and Oranim were forced to open their doors to all suitable applicants, not only kibbutz members.

This new situation required the introduction of a new pedagogical agenda and the academic adjustments required by the national teacher education program (Segal, 1972). After a period of pedagogical independence that lasted for approximately two decades, the kibbutz movement's teacher education apparatus found itself compromising its role as a radical educational alternative.

1980s–1990s: PROFESSIONALIZATION

During the 1970s and 1980s, a new professional academic trend emerged in Israeli teacher education (Ben-Peretz, 1991), which resulted in changes in the approach of the kibbutz movement. These changes were based on two key factors—the Americanization of Israeli society and international changes.

The Americanization of Israeli society, together with Israel's opening up to the world market and the cumulative impact of the 1967 and 1973 wars, brought far-reaching economic, social, and cultural changes to Israel society. While the standard of living of most Israelis rose, it was also possible to discern a retreat from the ethos of the pioneering society that had been prevalent during the first few decades of Israeli statehood. The political center was now penetrated by new forces that no longer regarded the kibbutz movement as an inspiring nation-building force, which it had been perceived to be during the early days of statehood. These social and political changes eroded the kibbutz movement's avant-garde self-perception and weakened the separatist orientation of its independent education system.

International changes resulted in a shift in pedagogical thinking in the Western world: In the United States, Cold War anxieties engendered a rise in the level of academic performance in schools based on standards of good teaching. The United States government provided the American education system with increased funding to lay a suitable foundation of scholarship for optimal teacher education. The goal was to understand how the teaching process worked and how it could be improved (Cochran-Smith & Fries, 2005; Darling-Hammond & Youngs, 2002; Fenstermacher, 2002).

The new approaches that evolved in the United States in the late 1960s found their way into Israeli teacher education in the 1970s, requiring increased disciplinary and occupational professionalization.

Decline of the Task-Focused Dimension and the Rise of Self-Fulfillment

The rising standard of living in Israel and Israeli society's opening up to the United States and Europe following the 1967 war had a profound impact on the kibbutz movement, which began abandoning its earlier socialist hyper-ideological models. The generation of children of the kibbutz movement founders now began calling into question the kibbutz's totalistic way of life and formative ideology:

> Now, and not only here—everything has collapsed. Among Stalin's bones, Herzl's beard, and the skeleton of the new man that is supposed to arise . . . we need not seek out a new philosophy but rather a new position, perhaps an anti-ideology of the current situation. . . . Our task today—the task of the young generation—is to build, on the foundation lay by the founding generation, a society in which every person can claim for himself, fulfill himself, and find his personality; a society of happy people, not of people sacrificing themselves on the altar. (Alon & Grossman, 1968, pp. 55–56, 70)

Members of the second generation sought new meaning and relevance for kibbutz life. They sought integration into Israeli public life, opposed the communal housing of kibbutz children in children's homes. Their rebellion also stretched to the anti-academic ethos of their parents, as they sought to enroll in university studies and not necessarily the purpose-focused kibbutz programs for teacher education.

These voices penetrated the two kibbutz campuses and also helped shape teacher education by weakening its political and ideological dimensions and enhancing its personality-related and instrumentalist dimensions. Still, the kibbutz movement left the administration of its two teacher education schools in the hands of kibbutz member general directors who replaced one another in rotation. Furthermore, despite its efforts to preserve certain unique elements of "collective education" within the subject matter taught, the trend of integration into national teacher education continued to intensify.

The year 1971 marked the establishment of University of Haifa's academic division at Oranim in the fields of the humanities and the sciences, enabling the institution to offer B.A. programs. A decade later, Seminar Hakibbutzim received accreditation to award B.Ed. degrees.

Uncomfortable Academization

In 1974, Seminar Hakibbutzim founding father Mordechai Segal was replaced by Shlomo Yitzhaki, but retained a joint governing council—consisting solely of kibbutz members—with Oranim. Yitzhaki, who forged a new relationship with the Ministry of Education, built the age-group tracks according to ministry guidelines. He also promoted the professionalization of the kibbutz teacher education schools on the pedagogical foundations of Benjamin Bloom (1956) and American behaviorist models, in accordance with the knowledge then being produced by Israeli universities.

The different geographical locations—Oranim in rural northern Israel and Seminar Hakibbutzim in urban Tel Aviv—and the character of the senior teaching staff resulted in different paths of adaptation at each of the two schools. Beginning in 1987, Seminar Hakibbutzim introduced workshops focusing on communication skills and reflective processes as a mandatory component of teacher education, using a large corps of psychologists, and declaring that their teaching was guided primarily by the pedagogy of caring (Noddings, 1984). The pedagogy of caring was rooted in the writings of Dewey, Buber, Korczak, and other thinkers who had influenced kibbutz education in its early days. In Israel's sociocultural context at the time, however, this psychologist form of teacher education received a new and very different translation, and did not take it upon itself to formulate a pedagogical alternative, as Seminar Hakibbutzim had done in its initial decades.

Conversely, Oranim was the site of very different attempts to preserve kibbutz education in the face of the "normalization" under way in the kibbutz movement and in reaction to the academization of teacher education in Israel. The two most prominent efforts in this direction were the establishment of the Midrasha in 1989 and the "Oranim Circle" (*Hug Oranim*) in the early 1980s.

The Midrasha connected students studying toward B.A. degrees and teaching certification in Jewish studies and the humanities with programs for the nonformal training of teens and young adults following their military service (Rabin Pre-Army Preparatory Program—*Mekhinat Rabin*). The Midrasha has focused on kibbutz society and the cultivation of pedagogical tools for nonformal education. Its ideological activity has nurtured the original kibbutz principle of the "unity of the forces of [kibbutz] education" and the kibbutz movement's desire of the 1960s and 1970s to "extend the age of the youth movement" spoken of in the kibbutz movement in the 1960s and 1970s (Dror, 2002, p. 14).

The Oranim Circle consisted of prominent charismatic academic lecturers from the fields of history and philosophy who attracted dozens of students who participated in dynamic discussion and activity groups. It was based on a theory for understanding politics that proposed Marxist political discussion and an analysis of society highlighting world financial forces, political alliances, and the different power systems that were ostensibly guiding political reality.

In the 1980s, the Oranim Circle had considerable influence on the young members of the kibbutz movement and on the efforts under way to intensify political education at Oranim as a legacy of original kibbutz education. A number of Oranim lecturers who were prominent ideological activists within both the Midrasha and the Oranim Circle lived on campus with their families. As a result of their close proximity to the student dormitories, the use of the main dining hall (which was also open in the evenings) by teachers and students alike, the campus's isolated location, and its profound sense of mission, Oranim emerged as an autonomous community and a sheltered ideological setting quite similar to the kibbutz itself. Perhaps this is why during the 1980s and 1990s the kibbutz movement regarded Oranim, and not its sister institution located in the urban center of Tel Aviv, as the preferable creative and ideological resource of kibbutz pedagogy.

2000–2015: THE "SECOND EDUCATIONAL WAVE" OF KIBBUTZ EDUCATION

The first decade of the twenty-first century in Israel was characterized by a government policy of cutting public expenditures on education and welfare. Politicians and the media charged teacher education in Israel, which accepted students with relatively low academic profiles, with training that was irrelevant to the challenges posed by the global community of knowledge, declining teacher performance on international examinations, and rising youth violence. Commissions were convened to address public demands made upon teacher education institutions to raise performance standards, intensify professionalization, and be more accountable (Ariav, 2006; Ben-Peretz Commission, 2001; Dovrat Commission, 2005). These commissions called for the increased academization of teacher education through more stringent acceptance requirements for teaching faculty, reinforcement of the component of discipline, and the grounding of training in current educational research.

Paradoxically, just when national demands were calling for teaching focused on instrumental goals subject to measurable standards, a brief but fascinating turn of events played out in the teacher education programs of the kibbutz movement's academic colleges. The developments were indicative of a desire to return to some of the foundations of progressive education and to reinforce the realms of social and political education. Seminar Hakibbutzim canceled most of its group dynamics lessons between 2003 and 2005 and, on the basis of this renewed social platform, opened its doors to "communal communities of educators" motivated by a sense of mission.

This new communal phenomenon, conducted by hundreds of members of the kibbutz movement's fourth generation and graduates of the youth movements run by and linked to the kibbutz movements, is dispersed throughout the entire country. Its unique manifestation is the urban kibbutzim established within socioeconomically weak development towns as declared educational goals ("educational kibbutzim"). These communal groups support themselves by providing educational services to youth movements in cities and kibbutzim, which can be defined as "supplementary education" (Michaeli, 2008).

In light of the radical processes of decline and transformation being experienced by kibbutzim today, these groups of young educators herald a new stage of development aimed at returning to the formative values of the kibbutz, while working to rectify their historical path and derive lessons from it. The "communal groups" are striving to establish ideological and economic independence and to return to the productive and nurturing activity that characterized the creative stage of the establishment of the kibbutz.

The unique pedagogy of the communal groups, which the education scholar Michaeli (2007) refers to as "social pedagogy," is similar to original kibbutz education in a number of respects. First, it offers an alternative approach to learning that blurs the dichotomy between formal and nonformal education, and between the elements of organization and content within the education system. Second, social pedagogy prioritizes "learning through engagement" and turns students into involved and productive partners in the instruction and learning processes. And finally, the members of the communal groups stress their commitment and the political purpose of the educational act, and, like the original kibbutz founders, regard themselves as establishing an all-encompassing and obligatory way of life. As they are engaged in education, these young adults approached the kibbutz movement colleges in pursuit of teacher training, with the aim of designing their program as a purpose-focused academic track consistent with their fundamental ideology.

At Oranim, the communal groups established ties with the teaching faculty of the well-established Oranim Circle, from which they drew inspiration primarily with regard to current sociopolitical analysis (Michaeli, 2007); in 2001, Seminar Hakibbutzim launched special training programs for these groups in postprimary humanities instruction (Yogev, 2011). The encounter with the groups' revived hyper-ideological conceptions posed a complex challenge for the teacher education program at Seminar Hakibbutzim, which had long since completed its academization. The groups embraced ideas that were dismissive of the hegemonic academic ethos, similar in spirit to the ideas that had motivated the founding generation of the kibbutz movement. In the words of one student:

> Entering academia is against our worldview. Academia is the temple of the hierarchy. . . . We have decided to embark on a purpose-focused academic track in academia. . . . We knew that they would be unable to accept all our terms. . . . We are not withdrawing our-

selves . . . but we want to shape it [the track] in our image. (Michaeli, 2007, pp. 378–380)

The encounter with these groups helped better clarify the college's sense of academic identity, highlighting just how far it had come and what it was no longer willing to give up. After a period of approximately one decade, the communal groups left Seminar Hakibbutzim and established an educational framework of their own at Beit Berl College, which provided them with organizational independence and academic autonomy.

In the years that followed, the impact of the communal groups' hyper-ideological orientation on the character of Seminar Hakibbutzim proved to be short lived. Their impact on the college's pedagogical agenda, however, has been significant, primarily as a result of the attention they drew to the need to enhance the social and political dimensions of kibbutz teacher education.

In 2007, the college established a Unit for Social Involvement to encompass the activity of the communal groups, which was granted the special budgetary authorization of the college management. Social involvement was now instituted as a mandatory part of the curriculum for all students and assigned three points of academic credit (School of Education, 2007; Yogev & Michaeli, 2011). Each week, college students make their way to troubled neighborhoods in cities such as Holon, Tel Aviv, Ramla, and Jaffa and play an active role in dozens of social organizations, welfare-based after-school programs for underprivileged children, and community centers. Their activity is supervised by designated faculty members and accompanied by sociological courses (School of Education, 2007).

The social-political dimension of teacher education was also expanded at Oranim. The Midrasha's guidance center continues to work with the nonformal education system, and some graduates of the Midrasha programs work there and make it a way of life, joining the communal groups and providing instructional and informal education services to schools and youth movements in cities and on kibbutzim.

The integration of the communal groups and youth into Beit Berl College within the School of People's Educators has unintentionally revived the historic alliance between the two kibbutz teacher education schools and Beit Berl College, which, until 1963, had been affiliated with the kibbutz movement as well. Now, however, it is Beit Berl that has positioned itself at the forefront of the hyper-ideological revival of the kibbutz idea by finding a place for the communal groups, with their unique training programs, and by integrating them into its ranks.

We can therefore understand the three formative hyper-ideological sources fueling the activity of the communal groups—their Zionist-socialist worldview, their collective lifestyle, and their efforts to establish a diverse movement of educators—as constituting a second life cycle of hyper-ideological kibbutz education. The first cycle took form with the establishment of the kibbutz and produced the comprehensive conception and unique practices of "collective education" during the first half of the twentieth century.

Beginning in the 1990s, in their unique manner, the communal groups have been reviving and rejuvenating the primordial kibbutz way of life and building a social pedagogy that suits it. Even if they constitute only a negligible minority on the margins of Israeli society, their very presence and work within the Israeli periphery and the national teacher training programs highlight the historic strength of kibbutz hyper-ideology and its unique educational heritage. Like the kibbutz during the first half of the twentieth century, these groups of educators are perceived of as making a unique contribution to Israeli society that is disproportionate to their actual number.

EPILOGUE

On February 8, 2015, Seminar Hakibbutzim and Beit Berl College signed an agreement consenting to their transfer from the responsibility of the Ministry of Education to the responsibility of the Council for Higher Education. According to the transfer agreement, the kibbutz colleges will be required to prove their ability to operate as economically and politically independent nonprofit organizations and to detach themselves from the kibbutz movement, which is defined as a self-interested economic and political corporation (and which controls more than 60 percent of the land on which the seminary is located).

The process of detachment began earlier, when the kibbutz movement sold a portion of the land on which the Tel Aviv campus of Seminar Hakibbutzim is located for private construction and used the lion's share of the proceeds to help settle the kibbutzim's debts and a smaller amount to build a new campus.

The kibbutz movement's willingness to sacrifice its unique seminaries as real estate, which, it was believed, would solve its complex financial problems, was also reflected in its relinquishment of the power to appoint the directors of the schools, which it enjoyed until 2012. The governing council, which had always been a joint body overseeing both institutions, was split in two and replaced, bringing an end to the two teachers' seminaries formal affiliation with the kibbutz movement.

For many decades, kibbutz hyper-ideology was perceived as articulating great meaning for those who espoused it. As we have seen, this ideology provided the founders of the kibbutz movement with substantial resources for the production of the extremely original pedagogy cultivated and promoted by the kibbutz approach to teacher education. Ultimately, however, this approach lost its ideological autonomy, causing it to quietly consent to the relinquishment of its independence and its role as a trailblazing alternative pedagogy.

This pessimistic conclusion, however, is challenged by the movement of the periodically rejuvenating life cycle of the remains of kibbutz education, which still appear to be vital and deeply rooted in the formative ethos of Israeli society.

As shown in this chapter, pedagogical frameworks displaying approaches and practices of kibbutz education as it developed since 1939 continue to operate at Oranim and Seminar Hakibbutzim (and now at Beit Berl College). In fact, 2016, when this chapter is being written, is the very year that the kibbutz movement relinquished its control over the kibbutz colleges: Seminar Hakibbutzim witnessed the establishment of a kibbutz education study group consisting of twenty-five academic faculty members. In addition, the college has renewed its cooperation with the Education Department of the Kibbutz Movement, which plays an active role in the training of administrators for educational institutions within the kibbutz sector and grants tuition scholarships to students who are also kibbutz members.

At Beit Berl College, the unique teacher training framework of the communal groups is thriving, and at Oranim the Rabin Pre-Army Preparatory Program and the Midrasha continue to attract the kibbutz's younger generation and Zionist youth movement graduates (Oranim, 2011). Even today, in contrast to other colleges in Israel, these three institutions—especially Seminar Hakibbutzim—conduct open and conscious social-political education within their teacher training programs (Yogev & Michaeli, 2011), while Oranim and Beit Berl maintain active frameworks for nonformal education that are infused with a sense of duty and mission.

Kibbutz pedagogy may have given up on being an alternative in teacher education. Nonetheless, some of its ideological values and even its practices have survived over the years in a fascinating life cycle and their influence on educational thinking in Israel is indelible.

NOTES

Prof. Esther Yogev was the provost of the Kibbutzim College of Education at Tel Aviv. She received her Ph.D. in history from Tel Aviv University and lectured at the Kibbutzim College of Education and in the History Department of Tel Aviv University. Yogev's current research examines the dilemmas facing history education in regions beset by unresolved ethno-political conflicts. E-mail: esther_yog@smkb.ac.il.

1. The Moshavim Movement is an organization consisting of 254 *moshavim* (plural of *moshav*, the Hebrew term for a specific type of cooperative settlement in Israel). It was established in 1953 to represent the unique interests of moshavim and Jewish agricultural villages in Israel relating to land rights and agricultural policy vis-à-vis various political institutions.

2. This isolationist approach was also presented vis-à-vis two other Zionist teachers' seminaries operating in Palestine's Jewish Yishuv at the time: the Levinsky Seminary, established in Tel Aviv in 1912, and the David Yellin Seminary, established in Jerusalem in 1914.

3. Proponents of the kibbutz idea proposed basing the education of children on a rational scientific system instead of erroneous parental intuition. Influenced by Freudian psychoanalysis, early theorists of collective education viewed the relationships within the traditional nuclear family as plagued by unsolvable conflicts. These conflicts could be avoided, they believed, by distancing the child from his or her parents (see Gerson, 1968; Golan, 1961).

REFERENCES

Alon, E., & Grossman, A. (Eds.). (1968). *A year after the war: Discussions by the younger generation*. June 5, 1968. Ein Shemer, Israel (Hebrew).

Ariav, T. (2006). *Tracing Training Guidelines for Teaching in Institutions of Higher Education in Israel—a Committee Report*. The Council for High Education (Hebrew).

Bartes, R. (1972). *Mythologies* (A. Lavers, Trans.). London, England: Paladin.

Bell, D. (1960). *The end of ideology: On the exhaustion of political ideas in the fifties.* Glencoe, IL: Free Press.

Ben-Peretz, M. (1991). The structure of knowledge as a guiding concept in curriculum development. In M. Zilberstein (Ed.), *The structure of knowledge of the disciplines: Implications for teacher education* (pp. 10–13). Jerusalem: Ministry of Education and Culture (Hebrew).

Ben-Peretz, M. (2008). *The lifecycle of reform in education from the circumstances of birth to the stages of decline: Causes, ideologies and power relations.* Based on an inaugural lecture delivered at the Institute of Education, University of London (June 19, 2007). London, England: Institute of Education, University of London.

Ben-Peretz Commission. (2001). *Teacher education in Israel and the changes of time: Report of the Commission to Examine Teacher Education in Israel.* Jerusalem: Ministry of Education (Hebrew).

Bloom, B. S. (1956). *Taxonomy of educational objectives.* Boston, MA: Allyn and Bacon.

Cochran-Smith, M., & Fries, K. (2005). Researching teacher education in changing times: Politics and paradigms. In M. Cochran-Smith & K. M. Zeichner (Eds.), *Studying teacher education: The Report of the AERA Panel on Research and Teacher Education* (pp. 69–109). Washington, DC: American Educational Research Association and Lawrence Erlbaum.

Darling-Hammond, L., & Youngs, P. (2002). Defining "high qualified teachers": What does "scientifically-based research" actually tell us? *Educational Researcher, 31*(9), 13–25.

Dovrat Commission. (2005). *The national program for education—Because every child deserves more: Recommendations of the National Taskforce for the Advancement of Education in Israel.* Jerusalem: Ministry of Education (Hebrew).

Dror, Y. (2002). *The history of kibbutz education: Practice into theory.* Tel Aviv, Israel: Hakibbutz Hameuchad (Hebrew).

Dror, Y. (2006). Settlement education at the beginning of the twenty first century. In A. Shapira (Ed.), *Ma'anit Halev: A tribute to Muki Tzur* (pp. 336–348). Tel Aviv, Israel: Hakibbutz Hameuchad, Yad Tabenkin (Hebrew).

Eagleton, T. (1991). *Ideology: An introduction.* London, England: Verso.

Fenstermacher. G. D. (2002). A commentary on research that serves teacher education. *Journal of Teacher Education, 53*(3), 242–247.

Foucault, M. (2002). *The archaeology of knowledge.* London, England: Routledge.

Gerson, M. (1968). *Education and family in the reality of kibbutz.* Tel Aviv: Sifriat Hapoalim (Hebrew).

Golan, S. (1961). *Collective education.* Merhavia, Israel: Sifriat Hapoalim (Hebrew).

Gouldner, A. (1976). *The dialectic of ideology and technology.* London, England: Macmillan.

Guess, R. (2001). *The idea of critical theory: Habermas and the Frankfurt School.* Cambridge, England: Cambridge University Press.

Hever Hakvutzot. (1951, November 21). Protocol of the Hever Hakvutzot Secretariat. (Hebrew).

Kafkafi, E. (1991). *A country searching for its people: Termination of the workers' stream of education.* Tel Aviv, Israel: Hakibbutz Hameuchad (Hebrew).

Kafkafi, E. (1998). Like olive saplings: "The Process Method"—The educational theory of Mordechai Segal and its application in the schools of the United Kibbutz Movement. *Dor Ledor, 12,* 259–286. Tel Aviv, Israel: Tel Aviv University (Hebrew).

Lyotard, J. F. (1999). *Postmodern fables.* Minneapolis: University of Minnesota Press.

Margolin, Y. (1957). *Nature education: The theory of Yehoshua Margolin.* Tel Aviv, Israel: Seminar Hakibbutzim Publications (Hebrew).

Michaeli, N. (2007). *People for tomorrow: The new Israeli communal groups—Intentional communities or signs of Labor Movement revival* (Unpublished doctoral dissertation). Tel Aviv University, Tel Aviv, Israel (Hebrew).

Michaeli, N. (2008). Creating the world you desire and live the world you create: Common attributes of the new communal groups. In Y. Dror (Ed.), *The communal groups in Israel* (pp. 477–522). Ramat Efal, Israel: Yad Tabenkin (Hebrew).

Noddings, N. (1984). *Caring: A feminine approach to ethics and moral education*. Berkeley: University of California Press.

Oranim. (2011, June). *The Spirit of Oranim: The magazine of Oranim College*. Oranim Archive (Hebrew).

Pavin, A. (2007). *The kibbutz movement: Facts and figures*. Ramat Efal, Israel: Yad Tabenkin (Hebrew).

School of Education. (2007). Protocol of the School of Education, the Kibbutz Teachers' Seminary, May 5 (Hebrew).

Segal, M. (1956, May 14). The tasks of education and teacher training. *Lamerhav* (Hebrew).

Segal, M. (1972). *The Kibbutz Teachers' Seminary in Tel Aviv: A survey in preparation for the founding meeting of the Academic Council, March 1972*. Segal's Papers: Kibbutzim College Archive (Hebrew).

Segal, M. (1992). *Ways of education*. Tel Aviv, Israel: Hakibbutz Hameuchad, with the support of the Kibbutz Teachers' Seminary, the Oranim Teachers' Seminary, and Yad Tabenkin (Hebrew).

Seliger, M. (1976). *Ideology and politics*. New York, NY: Free Press.

Seminar Hakibbutzim (2008, May 25). Protocol of the decisions of the School of Education (Hebrew).

Shils, E. (1968). The concept and function of ideology. *International Encyclopedia of the Social Sciences*, p. 7.

Timor, D., & Cohen, U. (2013). The attitude of the kibbutzim towards the institutions of higher education: From rejection and disagreement to integration. *Iyunim Bitkumat Israel, 23*, 378–410 (Hebrew).

Ya'ari, M. (1947). *On a long path: Premises, education, kibbutz, and society*. Merhavia, Israel: Hakibbutz Haartzi & Hashomer Hatzair (Hebrew).

Yogev, E. (2011). Back to the future: The dialectics of teacher education at the Kibbutz Teachers' Seminary and changes over time. In E. Yogev and R. Zuzovsky (Eds.), *Teacher education through the eyes of the researcher* (pp. 15–47). Tel Aviv, Israel: Hakibbutz Hameuchad and the MOFET Institute (Hebrew).

Yogev, E., & Michaeli, N. (2011). Teachers as society-involved "organic intellectuals": Training teachers in a political context. *Journal of Teacher Education, 62*(3), 312–324.

Yuval, A. (2015). Critical education and the twofold concept of ideology. In E. Yogev (Ed.), *Politics now: Enhancing political consciousness in high school* (pp. 1–13). New York, NY: Nova Science.

3

MONTESSORI IDEOLOGY AND PRACTICE IN TEACHER EDUCATION

Jacqueline Cossentino

Educators, of any persuasion, rarely consider themselves ideologues. While they might be comfortable with labels like "philosophical" or "principled," or even "visionary," they bristle at the notion that their action may somehow be governed by a rigid, predetermined pattern of thought. This is likely because ideology is so often associated with the negative side of a range of either/or propositions: belief versus evidence, opinion versus fact, propaganda versus truth, education versus indoctrination. Ideology is so often associated with oppression and false consciousness (Freire, 1970; Gramsci, 1971) that most practitioners view it as something to guard against.

Such binaries are overly simplistic and, more important, distorting when the subject is practice, especially educational practice. Ask a typical teacher why he or she entered the profession and most teachers will tell you they wanted to "make a difference." Some will say they "love children." Others will say they "love learning" (National Center for Montessori in the Public Sector, 2015). All of these answers reference life choices that are grounded in belief systems, which may be naive, but not surprising. If the critical theorists have made anything clear, it's that ideology is inescapable. All practice, particularly practice in schools, is ideological. All practice is value laden. All practice is grounded in conceptual frameworks and driven by beliefs.

This is an examination of how ideology informs the practice of Montessori education. Montessori education is grounded in a highly elaborate belief system, which guides practice, shapes culture, and endows the approach with an unusual degree of coherence (Cossentino, 2005, 2006, 2009). Part of what makes Montessori education so interesting is the manner in which its core assumptions about children and learning run counter to mainstream conceptions of teaching. Much of the power of Montessori seems counterintuitive, even paradoxical, to twenty-first-century (especially American) eyes.

The method's child-centered, discovery-oriented focus was revolutionary when it was first developed in the early part of the twentieth century. And while those same tenets render it, arguably, even more so today, critics sometimes dismiss the method as "old." Independence, freedom, and self-construction are core goals of the pedagogy, yet teacher practice is characterized by order, precision, and a meticulously practiced repertoire. And while its central purpose is to link healthy human development with social harmony and world peace, the boundary between Montessori insiders and outsiders is so starkly drawn that outsiders sometimes report feeling bewildered in Montessori circles (Bazelon, 2007).

These paradoxes, however, are precisely what make Montessori worth attention, especially when the subject is teacher practice. The method's insistent focus on meticulously detailed practice, guided by an elaborated theory of human development, which itself is grounded in a century of clinical observation, experimentation, and refinement, has produced what is likely the most stable, coherent, and scalable educational approach on the planet.

The paradoxes as well as the coherence are rooted in the method's history, a history that in some ways is typical of all educational movements and in other ways profoundly unique. The first Montessori school opened in 1907, as part of an urban renewal project in one of Rome's poorest neighborhoods, San Lorenzo. Designed originally to be a day care center housed on the ground floor of a housing project, the first *Casa dei Bambini* did not, at first, look much like the Montessori schools of today. Rather, the approach evolved based on Maria Montessori's ongoing observations of children's activity. Armed with a medical degree (along with its attendant skills in clinical observation),[1] Montessori engaged in ongoing experimentation with room organization, material design, groupings of children, use of time, and the behavior of adults.

By 1909, when the first training course was offered and she published her first book, Montessori had derived a set of insights from these experiments and formulated them into what she called "Scientific Pedagogy."[2] She continued to experiment for the rest of her life, making subtle adjustments, deriving new insights, and documenting the work in a set of lectures and writings, which now form the nexus of the Montessori knowledge base.

Though a product of rigorous academic training, Montessori, largely eschewed the academic world, which, typically, conferred legitimacy on educational approaches. As such, the method developed within an intimate circle of collaborators, particularly after 1918 when she left an academic appointment in order to devote herself entirely to the development of the schools that eventually came to bear her name. This circle formed the core of a community of practice that vigorously devoted itself to maintaining the method's integrity.

Over time, the community institutionalized and developed systems for codifying practice and reifying the theory undergirding that practice. This blend of historical continuity, cultural cohesion, and ideological coherence is unique among educational systems. No other system—not kindergarten, not progressive education (or any of its progeny)—has managed to remain recognizable in the face of the cultural and political forces that constantly exert themselves on schooling.

Montessori education is both scientific and ideological. Montessori ideology is, in fact, grounded in science, and empirical study of children in learning environments remains the cornerstone of the method. At the same time, Montessori culture has self-consciously organized itself around the goal of preservation. As such, it has evolved a discernable discourse, which is inherently ideological in ways that critics have sometimes viewed as "insular," "rigid," and "cultish" (Beck, 1961; Cohen, 1969). The central argument of this chapter, however, is that ideology operates in paradoxical ways within Montessori education. Moreover, the puzzles of Montessori ideology shed instructive light on not just the culture and practice of Montessori education, but how ideology works in practice, particularly the practice of teacher education.

IDENTITY, PRACTICE, AND DISCOURSE

Like the whole of Montessori culture, Montessori teacher education is distinguished by particular ways of thinking, talking, and doing. Montessori cultural practices are grounded in a "cosmological" worldview and enacted through ritualized interactions between teachers, students, and the learning environment (Cossentino, 2005). Moreover, within the Montessori worldview, healthy human development is directly linked to an optimistic vision of social reform fueled by compassion, respect for nature, and commitment to realizing human potential.

Montessori culture is also a global constellation of practice connected to thousands of local communities all sharing common values, rituals, and language, and all bounded by prescribed modes of participation. As such, Montessori culture typifies a "community of practice" (Wenger, 1998). Likewise, Montessori practice is governed by characteristic discourses, which enable Montessorians to establish boundaries between various modes of participation. Crossing those boundaries always involves training.

Montessorians share a common pedagogical repertoire, commitment to serving children through that repertoire, and spend a great deal of time engaged in activities that underscore the distinctiveness of their identity and practice as Montessorians. In fact, no other educational approach confers as much respect for pedagogical knowledge and skill, maps a direct path from novice to expert practitioner, or so confidently locates expertise at the core of its culture. Training is the path—the only path—leading one from peripheral to full participation in the Montessori community of practice (Cossentino, 2009; Whitescarver & Cossentino, 2007).[3]

Which is to say, one cannot claim to be a Montessori teacher simply by reading Montessori's writings or sensing an affinity with the philosophical tenets of the pedagogy. Rather, the process of becoming a Montessori teacher is embedded in both technical and theoretical mastery, which are, themselves embedded in practice.

Within Montessori culture, training is designed to be a transformative experience, in which one's thinking shifts not just in terms of classroom practice, but in terms of one's very orientation to relationships, environments, and human flourishing. Practice, moreover, is constituted in a complex blend of physical, intellectual, and spiritual activity.

One trainee describes it as "retraining." "Retraining your hand to do things and moving in a different way . . . It's not just learning. It's also how we move and how we speak. It's retraining yourself in general. It's changing yourself as a person."

The training explored here belongs to a particular segment of Montessori culture. The Association Montessori Internationale (AMI) was founded in 1929 by Maria Montessori for the express purpose of protecting the integrity of Montessori theory and practice. Though no longer the only Montessori association,[4] AMI holds unique status by retaining both the most direct link to the movement's founder and the most overtly global mission. Supported by three pillars: legacy, capacity, and outreach, AMI articulates an ambitious vision of social reform (outreach) grounded in the movement's century-long history of serving "the universal child" (legacy) through the training of teachers (capacity).

Until her death in 1952, Montessori personally oversaw (and in many cases delivered) all training across the globe. Following her death, her son Mario Montessori assumed leadership of AMI and, recognizing the fragility of a movement based on the genius of a single individual's ideas, devoted the remainder of his life to institutionalizing his mother's legacy. He focused on two elements of that legacy, both embodiments of Montessori's revolutionary ideas. First was the establishment of more schools in more places. Second, and even more important, was the preparation of a new generation of trainers to become the stewards of Montessori theory and practice. By the time of his death in 1982, a group of AMI trainers was firmly established as a robust and authoritative community of practice.

Today, the community of AMI trainers is, in many ways, the epicenter of AMI culture and practice. The trainers' influence is institutionalized in two discrete but overlapping subcommunities: the Scientific Pedagogy Group (SPG) and the Training Group (TG). The SPG approves course formats, provides advice and counsel on course readings and activities, and supervises the process of evaluating candidates for diplomas. Courses are numbered, diplomas are tracked, and originals cannot be replaced.

The Training Group oversees the selection and preparation of new trainers. More than any other segment of Montessori culture, the Training of Trainers program exemplifies the situated nature of Montessori learning—particularly teacher learning—and the manner by which community, identity, and learning coalesce in practice. Becoming a trainer entails "sitting" a minimum of two additional courses at the level at which the trainer will serve, preparing a set of lecture notes for subsequent courses, and apprenticing with experienced trainers. This process, which, typically, lasts for a minimum of three years and is almost entirely self-funded by the trainers in training, constitutes an extended induction into a rarified community of not just practice, but elders.

As an institution that values tradition and order, AMI observes a well-articulated status hierarchy and trainers reside at the top. Trainers hold seats on every major AMI committee, are featured speakers at every AMI gathering, and approve all major decisions related to pedagogy. As a culture entrusted with protecting the integrity of the Montessori knowledge base, AMI trainers are recognized as the brain trust of the movement. They are the wardens of an oral tradition that began with Maria Montessori's first lectures, is passed down from trainer to trainer, and disseminated through training courses, refresher courses, seminars, and congresses. And because the Montessori knowledge base is grounded in over a century of experimentation and self-scrutiny, trainers are also responsible for refining the articulation of theory and the implementation of practice. Trainers, thus, both embody and symbolize what is most important about Montessori culture, bearing standards of quality, guarding the boundaries that define various segments of Montessori culture, and shepherding participants across those boundaries.

THE MONTESSORI CENTER OF MINNESOTA [5]

The Montessori Center of Minnesota (MCM) is a comprehensive Montessori training center accredited by both AMI and the Montessori Accreditation Council for Teacher Education (MACTE). Like the mixed-age communities that comprise Montessori learning environments, Montessori training takes place in a developmental format divided into three- or six-year age spans. There are courses for 0–3, 3–6, 6–12, and 12–18. My observations and interviews all revolved around MCM's 3–6 course.

Since 1973, when MCM first opened its doors, the center has graduated 601 teachers. Today MCM is one of a handful of centers to provide a full preparation sequence from birth through age twelve.[6] It is also only one of two AMI training centers that colocates with a school. Since 2008, MCM has also been home to Montessori Partners Serving All Children, a network of affiliated Montessori programs serving vulnerable communities throughout the Twin Cities region. As such, MCM is recognized internationally for both training excellence and visionary implementation of Montessori's larger mission of social reform. MCM courses are consistently well subscribed,[7] graduates are both overwhelmingly satisfied with their experience and sought after for positions in schools all over the world. MCM's executive director and director of primary training, Molly O'Shaughnessy, is one of ninety-one trainers currently authorized by AMI as "full trainers."

THE PREPARED ADULT

Montessori teacher preparation differs substantially from conventional approaches to teacher formation. Montessori training courses have existed since 1909, when Maria Montessori offered her first training course at Villa Montesca, the Umbrian estate of Barone Leopoldo Franchetti and his American-born wife Alice Hallgarten Franchetti. Today, more than three hundred courses are offered on six continents. And while there is great variety among these programs, nearly all trace their origins back to Montessori's first courses and, as a result, share basic goals as well as structural elements.

Long before the image of practice as a triangle of interactions between students, teachers, and content was articulated by theorists like Sizer (1984) and Lampert (2001), Maria Montessori described the "method" as the triad of "a suitable environment, a humble teacher, and material objects adapted to their needs" (Montessori, 1966/1972, p. 137).

When prospective Montessori teachers take training, they learn that becoming a prepared adult means mastering different ways of interacting along the triangle. First is to prepare the learning environment so that it is ready for the child's constructive activity. Second is to interact with children in ways that invite rather than command engagement and,

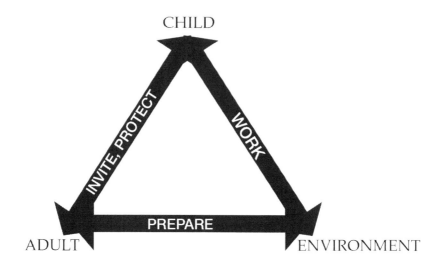

CHILD

ADULT

ENVIRONMENT

Figure 3.1.   The technical triangle of interactions between child, adult, and environment

third, once engagement is achieved, to protect the child's concentration.

AMI training courses outline three levels of preparation for the adult: physical, intellectual, and spiritual. Most courses are composed of five key elements: (1) lectures/demonstrations, (2) supervised practice, (3) material making, (4) clinical observation in Montessori classrooms, and (5) practice teaching. Lectures and demonstrations explicate the theory and practice of Montessori education, with special focus on the technical aspects of preparing an environment, presenting a lesson, daily observation, and facilitating classrooms in which most children are engaged in independent activity.

Supervised practice takes place in specially prepared practice rooms set up to mimic prepared environments for specific program levels. Practice rooms are both models of exemplary prepared environments and laboratories for trainees to explore the materials and rehearse presentations. From nomenclature cards, mystery bags, and object boxes in the early childhood environment to charts, timelines, and riverbed models in the elementary environment, teacher-made materials are a prominent part of Montessori environments at every level.

In AMI courses, observation is considered the cornerstone of the course and trainees spend a minimum of ninety hours observing in actual Montessori classrooms completing focused assignments on various aspects of interactions within the prepared environment. Finally, all AMI courses in the United States conclude with a period of teaching alongside an experienced teacher in an actual classroom.

As an AMI course, several elements of the MCM program are distinctive. First is the length and intensity of the experience. AMI courses are typically offered in one of two formats: Academic Year or Three Summers. The Academic Year format, which is what the trainees I studied here were engaged in, is nine months of six-hour days.[8] Early in the course, trainees spend two weeks (sixty hours) observing in Montessori classrooms. At the end of the course, they will spend six weeks practice teaching in similar environments. In between, most days are devoted to lecture/demonstration and practice.

Second, AMI training is always directed by a trainer who has completed the AMI Training of Trainers program. Completing the program qualifies the trainer to deliver all aspects of the course. Even in courses that are presented by more than one trainer (which is common in elementary programs), content is always presented as an integrated whole rather than a collection of subject-specific courses. Focus is on the child's experience of the environment with knowledge and skill transmitted in toto from expert to novice. Third is the creation of personalized manuals of all the lessons a teacher may present to children.

These manuals, called "albums," are typically composed of large three-ring binders filled with pages of lesson descriptions, illustrations, and presentation notes. A trainee in the Primary (3–6) course typically produces five such albums: Practical Life, Sensorial, Mathematics, Language, one for each area of the environment, plus an entire album devoted to Montessori theory. Write-ups are based on lesson demonstrations supported by media designed to capture the details of gesture as the trainer manipulates specific materials.

For most AMI Primary (3–6) diploma holders, albums represent close to a thousand pages of text. Trainees prepare their albums in stages, submitting sections for review throughout the course, and once completed, they are held—often treasured—as both reference tools and artifacts of the training process. Finally, in AMI courses, practice is emphatically framed by theory. The Theory Album is a collection of essays based on presentations and readings of Montessori's writings, most of which are transcribed lectures from earlier training courses. Here the language and logic of Montessori education are explicated: planes of development, sensitive periods, human tendencies, spontaneous activity, total reading and language explosions, the spiritual preparation of the adult.

At MCM the Theory Album is prepared throughout the course. In this way, the training mirrors the manner by which Montessori herself formulated the key concepts of the approach. Montessori theory emerged over time, through ongoing observation of children as they interacted with materials, with one another and with adults. More than any other educational approach, Montessori theory has been shaped by practice.

Vignette: The Practice Room

MCM shares space with a Montessori school[9] and a museum of Montessori history. On this particular afternoon, three days into the second semester and just about midway through a nine-month-long course, students are at work in MCM's Practice Room. Located next door to a media-equipped lecture room and down the corridor from a material-making studio, the Practice Room is set up as a classroom prepared to serve children between the ages of three and six.

This is a curated space, organized into discrete "areas" (Practical Life, Sensorial, Language, Mathematics), each with distinctive learning materials displayed on low shelves and in sequence from simple to complex. The walls are minimally adorned with framed fine art hung at child level. The bamboo floors are bare except for a few area rugs, which invite work with large, complex materials. Small tables, most of which are set for only one occupant, pepper the space. Fresh flowers in tiny vases, some placed on lace doilies, punctuate selected tables and shelves.

The "Practical Life" area includes, among other things, a child-sized ironing board and working iron, small glass pitchers for pouring both solids and liquids, fresh flowers and vases for flower arranging, and multiple trays equipped with materials for polishing shoes, wood, and silver. The Sensorial area is equipped with a variety of materials designed to support the refinement of sensorial discrimination. The various options—cubes, prisms, rods, cylinders with and without knobs, color tablets, smelling jars, tasting bottles, pitched bells, sorting trays—are all designed to isolate specific qualities (length, dimension, pitch, hue, savory, sweet, and so on) as well as provide "control of error," which enables children to correct themselves as they work with the material.

Close analysis reveals similarities between materials in different areas. The red rods, for instance, are a sensorial material designed to isolate the quality of length. They consist of ten wooden rods, all painted red, each differing in length by ten centimeters. They look a lot like the number rods, which are found in the Mathematics area and used for counting and understanding quantity. The number rods are identical to the red rods but are divided into red and blue sections. The shortest rod is red. The second is twice as long, with one half painted red and the other half blue. Prior to counting, the children use the red rods to explore the relationships between rods of different lengths. The two materials establish a concrete, sensorial link between ascending length and counting to ten, which the child experiences physically. By carrying each rod, number sense is, thus, embodied.

There are close to three hundred discrete items in this space and not a single piece is redundant or extraneous. Nearly all of the materials were originally developed in the early years of the twentieth century and, under the guidance of the Scientific Pedagogy Group, have been refined as needed based on painstaking monitoring and review. The number rods, for instance, were not always painted red and blue. Earlier versions (preserved in archives) were green and orange or blue and orange, and changes were decided based, in part, on how children responded to the material.

Today, the Practice Room is the site of work in the environment's Language Area. Molly has just completed a lecture on the function of words, a sequence of lessons that comes near the end of a child's stay in the 3–6 environment. The students have gathered in a circle around one of the small tables in the center of the room. There is a palpable hush as students prepare to observe Molly assume the role of the teacher while another student assumes the role of "child." There are no laptops in this space; trainees are expected to observe and, later, practice with full attention on the work with materials.

Once everyone is settled and the "child" has been identified, Molly walks over to one of the Language shelves and slowly, methodically, picks up a tray and carries it back to the table. The tray, known as the writing tray, is one of the items on a Montessori shelf that typifies the precision embedded in the method. It is a still life of written communication: a selection of perfectly sharpened pencils in one compartment, slips of paper in another, scissors, a role of tape, and a small basket for holding pieces of cut paper.

Slowly, deliberately, she pulls out the small chair, sits down at the table, choses a pencil and a strip of paper. She makes eye contact with the "child" seated to her right (Molly is left-handed), and carefully, slowly writes in cursive "the horse." The child reads the phrase, stands up, goes to the farm (a doll-house-sized model of an actual farm with a variety of animals, people, and structures), and brings back a horse. Molly says it is a nice horse, but not the one she was thinking of. She writes another clue on a separate slip of paper, "black." This additional word gives the child a sensorial impression of the adjective and its power to further describe which horse she was thinking about. The child reads the word and goes back to the farm and selects the black horse. The room is absolutely silent. When the child returns, Molly says, "Yes, that is exactly the horse I was thinking about" and then asks, "Would you like to do another?" And the process repeats, this time the slip refers to another animal from the farm. Molly uses the same purposeful movement and measured pacing. The child finds the particular animal and the process continues. At the conclusion of the second demonstration there is a pause for reflection, and both Molly and the child break character to debrief what has just been demonstrated.

One trainee notes that this exercise is similar to an earlier activity involving simple word recognition. Both entail "experiencing" language within the environment. Molly agrees and points out that function of words work comes at the point at which children are "pretty fluent readers," meaning their decoding skills are solid and thus they are able to experience the language emotionally. This, Molly explains, is the difference between mere "mechanical" and "interpretive" reading. After two more repetitions, the presentation concludes, with an invitation for students to spend what remains of the afternoon practicing.

Teacher Education from the Inside Out

What is, perhaps, most striking about the interactions described above is how deeply embedded they are in the details of practice (Ball & Forzani, 2009). Molly demonstrates the seamless interplay of thought and action entailed in this single sequence of activity—one of approximately four hundred that comprise the 3–6 pedagogical repertoire. Her students, meanwhile, attend to a thousand tiny details that govern those actions—how to arrange the writing tray, where on the shelf the tray should be placed, how to hold the pencil so as to model the proper grip, what sort of phrases to write on the slips, and how those phrases must match items that are present in the environment.

Like a clinical rotation in medical school, the trainees study every micromove that Molly demonstrates with surgical precision. They must absorb each move so that they can describe it in their albums and replicate it in their own practice. This technical work concentrates intensively on the hows of practice: how to speak, how to walk, sit, and stand, how to push in a chair, organize materials, fold a piece of cloth, sew a placemat, how to modulate voice pitch and tone. Trainees describe this aspect of their preparation as the most difficult part of the experience. Many, from a variety of courses, have told me it was "the hardest thing I've ever done." The difficulty stems from what one trainee described as the discipline required to "watch all those presentations, and do all the write-ups," many of which are "repetitive" and, for some, "tedious." Discipline and repetition are understood to be part of the process. "We were told to trust the process," that same trainee explained.

The "process" here refers to the work of developing a teaching repertoire that is both richly detailed and highly flexible. Unlike conventional teacher preparation, where the details of practice are often left to the individual teacher to formulate and personalize, Montessori training presents aspiring teachers a complete pedagogical repertoire: a canon developed and refined over time by experts through a century of systematic internal scrutiny. Supported by the authority and stability of this canon, Montessorians build their practice from the inside out. Though not entirely a linear process, it is fair to say that doing precedes thinking; action leads to theory. Technical mastery provides the scaffolding upon which to support the development of a deep, flexible practice that is driven by children's needs rather than curricular mandates.

For instance, implicit in Molly's demonstration is an appreciation of the child's readiness to explore the function of words. He must be "a pretty fluent reader" and, therefore, ready to move beyond "mechanical" reading or decoding and toward what Montessorians refer to as "total reading."[10] Also implicit is an understanding of the manner in which children between the ages of three and six optimally learn. The preparation of an environment that is rich but uncluttered is grounded in an appreciation of the importance of concentration in learning.

Likewise, emphasizing student choice within a highly organized environment or, as Montessorians call it, "freedom within limits," encourages independence, which is necessary for both self-direction and adaptability. The precision with which Molly demonstrates the handling of the tray, pencil, and slips is designed to respond to the young child's sensitivity to order. And the notion that the child's emotional response to written communication is a necessary element of learning to read—what Montessori called "reading explosions." While the trainees' Theory Albums will contain explications of Montessori's own formulations of the concepts of sensitive periods, concentration, independence, freedom within limits, and total reading, those concepts come to life in the Practice Room.

Like the child who must experience an idea before internalizing its definition, trainees internalize their repertoire by tacking back and forth between lecture/demonstration, observation, and practice. Like the development of Montessori theory itself, the trainees' understanding of the whys of Montessori practice emerges over time, always within the context of ongoing rehearsal of the hows and always in reference to children.

If the hows of Montessori practice constitute the technical aspect of training, and the whys the theoretical, a third aspect, the what fors, move closer to the ideological: "This is not merely a question of learning something. It is a question of achieving a revolution within ourselves and of our whole outlook, of our whole attitude, of everything we are" (Joosten, 1971, p. 12). The "revolution" that AMI trainer Albert M. Joosten (1914–1980) describes above captures the essence of what Montessorians frequently describe as the "transformation" training aims to induce. Full participation in Montessori culture is as much a matter of identity as knowledge and technique. The unusually tight alignment between the hows, whys, and what fors of Montessori practice constitutes a "cosmological" worldview (Cossentino, 2005).

As the figure below illustrates, Montessori cosmology embeds the technical aspect of practice within the theoretical, which itself is enveloped in a comprehensive vision of a better life. The logic of this system is clear: When learning is designed to respond to the natural tendencies and needs of human development, children thrive, and when children thrive, they grow to be self-directed, compassionate human beings, who are able to achieve order and harmony in their lives, which can, eventually, enable social progress toward peace.

The internal consistency evidenced in Montessori cosmology stands in stark contrast to prevailing conceptions of teaching practice as eclectic and uncertain (Helsing, 2007; McDonald, 1992). The system, however, is precisely what enables Montessori practitioners, novice as well as expert, to experience the "transformation" that Joosten describes.

As Andrews (2013) explains, transformation is the result of preparation that intentionally links "physical, intellectual and spiritual" dimensions of practice, which in the training are "integrated through experience with children" (p. 3). Sometimes referred to as "inner preparation"

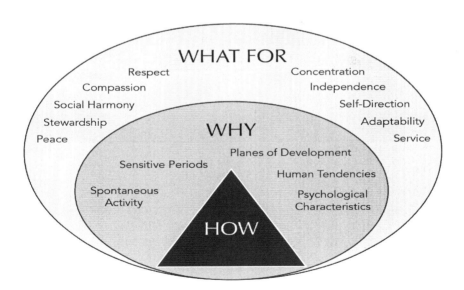

Figure 3.2.   Montessori cosmology

(Montessori, 1939/1998, p. 104) or "the training of one's self" (Montessori, 1967, p. 132), the spiritual preparation of the adult signals a comprehensive shift not just in thinking and doing, but also in belief and attitude or what are sometimes called "dispositions" (Whitescarver & Cossentino, 2007). Transformation, in other words, is the result of a fully integrated worldview in which the hows, whys, and what fors of education align in ways that shift the trainees' thinking not just about being a particular kind of teacher, but also about being a particular kind of person.

IDEOLOGY IN ACTION: EMBODIED PRINCIPLES

Whether referred to as a "framework," "cosmology," "worldview," or "discourse," the goal of this chapter is to capture the manner by which action and intention cohere. Gee's (1990) formulation of Discourse provides a useful lens for analyzing the manner by which Montessori practitioners—trainers as well as trainees—through both talk and action embody core precepts of Montessori cosmology. In Gee's formulation, a Discourse (as distinct from discourse) is "a sort of 'identity kit,' which comes complete with the appropriate costume and instructions on how to act, talk, and often write, so as to take on a particular social role that others will recognize" (p. 142). In other words, being "trained" as a Montessori 3–6 teacher means learning how to speak, think, and act like a Montessorian.

Or as Molly puts it, "To truly serve their [children's] needs we always have to go back to principles." Talk of "principles," in fact, dominated conversation with everyone I met at MCM. Molly and Connie in particular continually used the term whenever they talked about their work, both with trainees and with other audiences, particularly those associated with Montessori Partners Serving All Children. In highlighting the importance of "principles" to the trainees, Molly refers to the dictionary definition: "A principle," she explains, "is a fundamental truth or belief that exercises a directing influence on life and behavior." For Molly and Connie (and now the trainees), Maria Montessori is the source of multiple "fundamental truths," and a central task of training is to integrate these truths so that the trainee becomes "deeply steeped in the principles and ideals."

These "principles and ideals" are fully elaborated in Montessori cosmology and recognizable in the Discourse of Montessori practice. Within the Discourse of Montessori practice more discrete discourses or "social languages" operate. Social languages/discourse are part of Discourses, but are constituted in language only. Practitioners use these social languages, with varying degrees of fluency, to make sense of the relationship between the hows, whys, and what fors of Montessori practice. At MCM, three particular discourses were used by trainers and trainees to "steep" themselves in Montessori principles.

Human Potential

Human potential discourse revolves around the core concept of development and deals principally with the connection between the whys and what fors of Montessori practice. Montessori pedagogy begins with a deep study of human development, which Montessori mapped as occurring in stages. Foreshadowing Piaget's stage theory, Montessori identified four successive stages or "planes" of development (Birth–6, 6–12, 12–18, 18–24), each with distinctive characteristics and tendencies. Supporting the realization of human potential requires close study of the child and the preparation of learning environments specifically designed to meet the needs of children at each stage of development.

Talk of human potential is ubiquitous in Montessori culture. In addition to providing a title for one of Montessori's texts,[11] the term appears often as a shorthand for goals of the approach. Whenever someone invokes concepts of independence, personalization, human needs, or nature, they are engaging in the human potential discourse. A trainee explained her own early engagement with this discourse when she told me about a theory lecture on human needs and tendencies that "really opened [her] eyes: There were so many of them that I have never paid consideration to before. The fact that we're noticing those, and we're looking for those, so we can support children, so they can grow into well-rounded people and serve the world." Here, this novice practitioner—less than halfway through her training—maps a direct relationship between the observed needs and tendencies of young children, appropriate educational supports, and well-rounded human beings.

Within Montessori cosmology, human development is, foremost, a natural process, the disruption of which is the cause of problems. "One of the biggest truths," Molly explains, "is that we are not in charge. Nature is." Here, she underscores the difference between Montessori and conventional understandings of human development. Conventional teachers may think they are in control, but "we" know better. She continues, "We need to read from the book of nature; and not only for our relationship with children, but with everything in the universe. We are all," she emphasizes, "connected." Here, she links the whys of Montessori practice to the what fors: human development is natural; a robust understanding of which will support the "our" task of being an aide rather than an obstacle, which will, in turn, foster self-assured people of service and a deeper awareness of cosmic unity.

Love

Within Montessori cosmology, love is usually more evident in actions than in words. Teachers act out love when they prepare environments that foster concentration and independence, refrain from interrupting children who are engaged in work, observe children in order to better understand their needs and tendencies, and use a soft, neutral voice in conversation. Molly articulates a similar kind of love for her trainees when she tells them, "Staff have taken a lot of time and put a lot of love and care into preparing this environment for you so that you would feel comfortable, safe, oriented—so that you knew where things were. This training environment for you is a place to facilitate your own growth. We hoped you'd fall in love with it, that you would come to see it as a special place for you." Love, here, is constituted in the physical (and attending emotional) space deliberately prepared to support development.

When Connie talked about "human relationships" and qualities necessary to nurture healthy relationships, whether between children and adults, trainees and trainers, or parents and teachers, she consistently emphasized empathy, respect, and humility. As the director of outreach programs, Connie spends a great deal of her time interacting with untrained people—policy makers, local leaders who are just learning about Montessori, and parents who, sometimes, are just trying to make it through the day. She regards of these people as "partners," and considers all of her interactions to be extensions of her Montessori practice. "It's a whole lot of intentional listening, a lot of question asking. Rather than observing a relationship and going 'oh boy do you have problems; let me tell you how to fix this,' we just listen. And we watch. And by doing so, we empower our partners to discover for themselves what their questions are. And once they ask, then we have things to offer."

She is talking about adults here, but the message is wholly consistent with how any trained Montessorian would describe the delicate process of inviting a child to engage, then patiently waiting for interest to arise so that real learning can begin. Coming to understand that love is a practice rather than an emotion, that loving children has more to do with assisting them in realizing their potential than with expressing affection, and that love is made visible not in hugs but in work is central to the process of becoming trained.

Craft

If Montessori education is a practice of love aimed toward realizing human potential, one learns that practice through an intensive immersion in the details of technical knowledge. This craft orientation highlights a seminal difference between Montessori teacher preparation and other models (Cossentino, 2009). Where conventional teacher education aims to provide multiple perspectives on learning—behaviorism, constructivism, play-based, project-based—Montessori situates the practice of teaching (and learning) within a singular worldview. The idea that technical knowledge is embedded in theoretical knowledge, and that both are mastered through rigorous, repetitive practice is so central to Montessori teacher education that it is has come to define the very meaning of the training experience.

By contrast, the "survey" approach to teacher education offers an "objective" rather than "ideological" approach to teacher formation, presumably, so students can decide for themselves how they will orient their practice. But in Montessori teacher education, objectivity is not the point. Instead of offering a collection of theories to pick and choose based on preference or personality, Montessori training provides a comprehensive worldview in which all elements of theory and practice cohere. To be trained is to be fluent in the language and logic of that worldview, which is only achieved through immersion.

Likewise, the experience of becoming a trainer is deeply grounded in the craft tradition of apprenticeship. Through multiple cycles of observation, rehearsal, and reflection, trainers in training move toward full participation in the AMI trainer community of practice. To some extent the process resembles the apprenticeship journey of graduate students headed toward professorship. But there is no analogue in traditional teacher education. This is the result of a knowledge base for teaching that remains contested and uncertain (Heibert, Gallimore, & Stigler, 2002). By contrast, the Montessori knowledge base is both codified and situated in its cosmological view of practice.

CONCLUSION: GROUNDED IDEOLOGY

This chapter has aimed to demonstrate the unique way in which ideology operates within Montessori teacher training. In weaving together practice, community, and worldview, Montessori training provides not just a revised pedagogical script, but a wholly new discourse of education. That discourse replaces the dominant discourse of education as achievement with a cosmological view of education as the realization of human potential. Training constitutes the commencement of a lifelong engagement that grants access to both local and global communities of practice.

To say that Montessori education is ideological is to recognize that few, if any, other educational approaches are governed by such a coherent system of thinking and doing. Moreover, to say that Montessori is both grounded in science and driven by principles is to identify a paradox that is only puzzling to those beyond the Montessori world. AMI trainers, in particular, embody a fully and intentionally integrated ideology of education for human potential. As one of Molly's trainees observed, "She really embraces it all: And so to the core. She's not just teaching a class. She totally encompasses the entire Montessori belief and practice. To me, I walk away from the lecture and think, someday I wanna be like you." Functioning as masters of the technical, intellectual, and spiritual dimensions of Montessori practice, trainers both preserve and transmit the core of Montessori culture.

This close look at how Montessori ideology operates within Montessori teacher training also helps illuminate some of the other paradoxes of Montessori education. Most notable is the manner by which Montessori practice manages to be both highly structured and student centered. In its emphatic emphasis on the hows of practice, it would be easy to conclude that Montessori practice aims toward a rigid, mechanical approach to instruction. However, as Connie and Molly emphasized repeatedly, the technique is only as useful as the principles that guide it.

The hows of Montessori practice, in other words, only make sense when they are clearly and seamlessly linked to the whys and what fors. Montessori teacher training makes that link explicit and, in so doing, claims a powerful and, arguably, essential role for ideology in professional formation.

NOTES

1. Montessori was also deeply influenced by the work Jean-Marc-Gaspard Itard and Éduoard Séquin, two of the grandfathers of special education.

2. *Il Metodo della Pedagogia Scientifica applicato all'educazione infantile nelle Case dei Bambini*, eventually translated to *The Montessori Method*.

3. There are many ways to participate in Montessori culture without being trained. My own experience as, first, an untrained school administrator and, more recently, a leader of a national support organization, has granted me access to many "insider" communities. Yet, without a Montessori diploma, I am not able to prepare environment, give lessons, or attend certain meetings.

4. Today dozens of Montessori associations operate, and two major organizations dominate the Montessori movement worldwide. Alongside AMI, the American Montessori Society (AMS) was founded in 1960 by a group of American Montessorians whose chief goal was to bring Montessori education to large numbers of students and educators. AMS's emphasis on expansion is reflected in its status of the largest Montessori organization currently operating. Both organizations sponsor training programs, and both have a global presence, though AMS dominates in the United States.

5. The author is grateful to the staff of the Montessori Center of Minnesota, particularly Molly O'Shaughnessy and Connie Black, for their participation in this investigation, and for their sensitive feedback on earlier versions of this chapter.

6. The 0–3 or "Assistants to Infancy" course is offered occasionally; while the 3–6 (Primary) and 6–12 (Elementary) are offered annually.

7. At least twenty students.

8. This particular course was modified to run from one to six each day in order to provide trainees the opportunity to use their mornings for work, additional study, or other activities.

9. Cornerstone Montessori is the flagship, laboratory school that anchors Montessori Partners Serving All Children.

10. What Montessori called "total reading" refers to the combination of fluency, comprehension, and emotional response necessary for the reader to fully experience text as meaningful communication.

11. *To Educate the Human Potential* was first published in 1948 "to help teachers to envisage the child's needs after the age of six" (Montessori, 1948/1973).

REFERENCES

Andrews, S. W. (2013). *The Montessori adult.* Portland, OR: Montessori Northwest.

Ball, D. L., & Forzani, F. (2009). The work of teaching and the challenge for teacher education. *Journal of Teacher Education, 60*(5), 497–511. doi:10.1177/0022487109348479

Bazelon, E. (2007). The cult of the pink tower: Montessori turns 100—What the hell is it? Slate. Retrieved August 15, 2009, from http://www.slate.com/id/2166489/

Beck, R. (1961). Kilpatrick's critique of Montessori's method and theory. *Studies in Philosophy and Education, 1*(4–5), 153–162.

Cohen, S. (1969). Maria Montessori: Priestess or pedagogue? *Rec, 71*(2), 313–326.

Cossentino, J. (2005). Ritualizing expertise: A non-Montessorian view of the Montessori method. *American Journal of Education, 111*(2), 211–244. doi:10.1086/426838

Cossentino, J. (2006). Big work: Goodness, vocation, and engagement in the Montessori method. *Curriculum Inquiry, 36*(1), 63–93. doi:10.1111/j.1467-873X.2006.00346.x

Cossentino, J. (2009). Culture, craft, & coherence: The unexpected vitality of Montessori teacher training. *Journal of Teacher Education, 60*(5), 520–527. doi:10.1177/0022487109344593

Freire, P. (1970). *Pedagogy of the oppressed* (Revised ed.) New York, NY: Continuum.

Gee, J. (1990). *Social linguistics and literacies: Ideology in discourses.* Philadelphia, PA: Falmer Press.

Gramsci, A. (1971). *Selections from the prison notebooks* (Q. Hoare & G. N. Smith, Trans.). New York, NY: International.

Heibert, J., Gallimore, R., & Stigler, J. (2002). A knowledge base for the teaching profession: What would it look like and how can we get one? *Educational Researcher, 31*(15), 3–15.

Helsing, D. (2007). Regarding uncertainty in teachers and teaching. *Teaching and Teacher Education, 23*(8), 1317–1333. doi:10.1016/j.tate.2006.06.007

Joosten, A. M. (1971). *The spiritual preparation of the adult.* Lecture delivered at the Indian Montessori Center.

Lampert, M. (2001). *Teaching problems and the problems of teaching .* New Haven, CT: Yale University Press.

McDonald, J. (1992). *Teaching: Making sense of an uncertain craft.* New York, NY: Teachers College Press.

Montessori, M. (1939/1998). *Creative development in the child* (Vol. 2) (R. Ramachandran, Ed.). Madras, India: Kalakshetra Publications.

Montessori, M. (1948/1973). *To educate the human potential.* Madras, India: Kalakshetra Publications.

Montessori, M. (1966/1972). *The secret of childhood.* New York, NY: Ballentine Books.

Montessori, M. (1967). *The absorbent mind.* Madras, India: Kalakshetra Publications.

National Center for Montessori in the Public Sector. (2015). Survey of Montessori Teacher Trainees. Washington, DC: NCMPS.

Sizer, T. (1984). *Horace's compromise: The dilemma of the American high school.* Boston, MA: Houghton Mifflin.

Wenger, E. (1998). *Communities of practice: Learning, meaning, and identity.* Cambridge: Cambridge University Press.

Whitescarver, K., & Cossentino, J. (2007). Lessons from the periphery: The role of dispositions in Montessori teacher training. *Journal of Educational Controversy, 2*(2). Retrieved from http://cedar.wwu.edu/jec/vol2/iss2/11

4

WHAT CAN TEACHER EDUCATORS LEARN FROM REGGIO EMILIA AND PISTOIA, ITALY?

Lella Gandini and Carolyn Pope Edwards

Teaching practices in the public early childhood programs of north and central Italy have inspired others from around the world for their sustained high level of quality. As a result, Italian educators—especially those from renowned systems of Reggio Emilia, Pistoia, and other progressive cities—are frequently asked, "How are teachers prepared and supported to work in such competent ways in preschools and infant-toddler centers?"

Based on years of study and interaction, this chapter describes and analyzes the processes of preservice preparation and in-service professional development in Reggio and Pistoia. These two cases offer different, but complementary, examples of how Italians from regions with enlightened political environments have created strong, city-run systems for educators to prepare themselves and continually improve their daily work. They illustrate how sustained, coconstructive, reflective practice provides a coherent approach to systemic quality that derives neither from imported models nor from imposed quantitative assessment, but from intellectual resources generated within and between broad communities of committed professionals.

In this progressive Italian way of thinking about teacher preparation and professional development, what comes first is a vision of the elements of quality in early childhood services, a vision largely shared throughout the country (Fortunati, 2007). What comes second is a set of organizational and pedagogical strategies for the ongoing preparation and continuous improvement of teachers' knowledge, skills, and dispositions for working with children and families (Lazzari, Picchio, & Balduzzi, 2015; Lazzari, Picchio, & Musatti, 2013). Accordingly, the visions from Reggio Emilia and Pistoia are first presented, followed by a description of the system of preservice early childhood teacher preparation applied throughout Italy, and then discussion of the processes for in-service teacher professional development in Reggio and Pistoia. The chapter concludes with some comments on the similarities and contrasts between the two cases.

A VISION OF CONTINUAL GROWTH FOR TEACHERS IN REGGIO EMILIA

Reggio Emilia is a city in northern Italy where a volunteer group of educators, parents, and children came together after World War II with a shared vision for a new kind of school for young children (Edwards, Gandini, & Forman, 1993, 2012). Under the leadership of the founding director, Loris Malaguzzi (1920–1994), the system then evolved from a parent cooperative movement into a city-run system of first preschools and then also infant-toddler centers. The system exercises a leadership role in educational innovation in Italy and Europe, and now increasingly the world.

The Reggio Emilia approach is not an educational model in the formal sense, with defined methods, teacher certification standards, and accreditation processes. However, over the past sixty years, educators there have evolved distinctive strategies to foster children's intellectual development through a focus on symbolic expression. Young children (from birth to age six) are encouraged to explore their environment and express themselves through many "languages," or modes of expression, including words, movement, drawing, painting, sculpture, shadow play, collage, music, and photography and digital media. Leading children to surprising levels of symbolic skill and creativity, the system is not private and elite but rather involves full-day child care open to all, including children with disabilities.

Lella Gandini asked Loris Malaguzzi, founder, "You said that teachers should also be researchers; how do you promote this in your schools?" He replied, "There is no choice but continuous professional development." At that time, early childhood teacher preparation in the high schools and colleges did not meet the rising expectations of the emerging public early childhood system in Reggio.

Loris Malaguzzi believed that teachers, like children and everyone else, feel the need to grow in their competencies because they seek to become active interpreters of what is happening in their classrooms. They want to "transform experiences into thoughts, thoughts into reflections, reflections into new thoughts and new actions. They also feel a need to make predictions, to try things out, and then interpret them. The act of interpretation is most important. Teachers must learn to interpret ongoing process, rather than wait to evaluate results" (Gandini, 2012a, pp. 48–49). Malaguzzi went on to say,

> Teachers must be aware that practice cannot be separated from objectives or values and that professional growth comes partly through individual effort but in a much richer way through discussion with colleagues, parents and experts. . . . [I]t is not possible even to begin if teachers do not have a basic knowledge about various content areas of teaching in order to transform this knowledge into 100 languages and 100 dialogues with children. We have at present limited means to prepare teachers as we would like, but we try to look within ourselves and find inspiration from the things we do. (Gandini, 2012a, p. 49)

Clearly, an ideal of interdisciplinary dialogue and exchange is embedded in these words. Malaguzzi wanted teachers to have the capacity to transform their basic academic content knowledge into "100 languages" and "100 dialogues with children." By this, he metaphorically offered a vision about the ongoing professional development of teachers of young children that has an open door to other cultural aspects such as poetry, theater, art, design, photography, cinema, the culinary arts, and more. He also believed that teachers should encounter the most advanced research in education and child psychology and become aware of new theories (Mantovani, 1998).

Malaguzzi's intention was to suggest that teachers could develop new insights and see with "new eyes" and act with "new hands," that is, on the basis of fresh observations and practices, and thus move beyond the limiting educational traditions that dispossess children of their own eyes and hands. Teachers need new perspectives that they can discuss with their colleagues and figure out together how to offer richer resources to children. "If the heads think, then hands also have to think," he used to say, meaning that teacher reflection should extend to what teachers *do* as well as what they *think* and *say*.

In the beginning days, the leaders in Reggio Emilia were working against the tradition of educating young children based on teacher-centered practices, simple routines, and prescribed repetitive games, rather than exploration of materials and the environment in creative ways and representing them with expressive tools and materials. The innovative municipal early childhood system in Reggio (as in other cities) was also discontinuous with the elementary school system, governed by the national Ministry of Education (Edwards, Gandini, & Forman, 2012).

Starting in the late 1980s, the world began to discover that there was an experience of great interest developing in Reggio Emilia. It was not a "method," but rather an "approach," a general way of thinking, observing, discussing, projecting, and experimenting. This approach was always to be rooted in the local context. It was not based on a set curriculum or predefined path, but rather on critical, open-minded scrutiny of the quality of environment, materials, and interactions—a continuous research, construction, and reconstruction of knowledge made visible through observation and documentation (Edwards & Gandini, 2015; Edwards, Gandini, & Nimmo, 2015).

Malaguzzi had a brilliant flair for metaphor and often drew on well-known literary and cultural references to make a point. He especially liked the myth of "Ariadne's thread," coming from the Greek myth about the king of Minos and his beautiful daughter, Ariadne, who was in love with the hero Theseus. Ariadne wanted to help Theseus slay the Minotaur, a terrifying monster imprisoned under the city. Ariadne used her intelligence and resourcefulness to help Theseus find his way through the maze in which the Minotaur was held. Ariadne gave Theseus a ball of yarn so he could find his way out once he had slain the Minotaur.

Therefore, by making reference to "Ariadne's thread," Malaguzzi was speaking of a smart woman finding a clever solution in a difficult and obscure situation. He made a comparison to the complex work of the teacher who also is capable of drawing on her own intelligence to solve complex problems and offer "threads" or "pathways" to make the teaching and learning process positive for children and families.

Carlina Rinaldi was once a *pedagogista* (pedagogical coordinator), later became president of Reggio Children, and now serves as president of the Reggio Children Loris Malaguzzi Centre Foundation. According to Rinaldi, Loris Malaguzzi had wanted our book *The Hundred Languages of Children* to be named instead after Ariadne's thread, dedicated to all the teachers of Reggio Emilia (Rinaldi, 1998). Vea Vecchi, longtime *atelierista* at the Diana School, talked about this myth while wandering with Lella through the exhibit *Il filo d'Arianna (Ariadne's Thread)*, a revisitation of the documentation of the Reggio infant-toddler centers and preschools from 1981 to 2008, then on display in the Loris Malaguzzi International Center. Vecchi said that in the 1980s, they were already thinking that even a small thing contains great complexity, just like a large thing, and that the complexity of a small subject can be brought out and interpreted with children (Gandini, 2012b, pp. 314–315).

THE VISION OF CONTINUAL GROWTH FOR TEACHERS IN PISTOIA

An alternative image of the early childhood teacher arose in Pistoia (Galardini & Giovannini, 2001). Pistoia is another Italian city in which educators, public officials, parents, and ordinary citizens have worked together to build systems of high-quality, public services to support and serve young children and their families. While Reggio Emilia continues to receive the highest level of international recognition, these other localities are also acknowledged sites of important leadership and experimentation (Gandini & Edwards, 2001).

Pistoia, in the central Italian region of Tuscany, has put forward a strong concept of the responsibility of public administration to create ways and means to enhance family participation in educational services. Pistoia has pioneered a system of diverse services and resources to reach out across the generations and segments of the city and communicate children's needs and a positive view of childhood. The public early childhood system includes traditional preschool and infant-toddler centers; part-time parent-child programs; after-school enrichment classes; and *Area Bambini* (Children's Areas) that specialize in diverse programming around domains such as parent-infant relationships, storytelling and oral tradition, nature and environment, computers and technology, and the visual and manual arts.

The general philosophical and pedagogical outlook in Pistoia is congruent with that of educators in Reggio Emilia, but aspects of implementation differ, and as in Reggio, are always evolving over time. For example, in Pistoia there are more part-time programs for toddlers, based on Pistoia's desire to provide services to nonworking mothers.

Annalia Galardini, the founding director of Pistoia's municipal early childhood programs, sometimes describes the image of the "empathic educator" as central to the vision of quality in children's services. As the teacher plays the role of "partner in play," she can develop an attitude of empathy toward children—not too demonstrative, not too cold and indifferent. Empathy means the "right time." "When we share daily life with children and, in particular when we share moments of play, the important thing is to encounter one another, listening without misunderstanding, without overriding the other's meaning, in harmony based on deep, mutual familiarity" (Galardini & Giovannini, 2001, p. 98).

Galardini also views *empathy* as central to her moral ideal of administrative leadership (Edwards & Gandini, 2001, p. 197). As a leader, Galardini models the kind of empathic, compassionate attitude that she believes should shape all relationships in the system, including relations among children. The same is true for the three lead administrators of the Pistoia early childhood system whose complementary talents enabled them to depend on one another utterly and to work together well and support each other.

Donatella Giovannini, pedagogical coordinator, believes that in her city, teachers as professionals must be able to construct, with support, new pedagogical knowledge and question themselves as developing persons. They have to value their own gifts and abilities, be ready to face complex situations, and have their own cultural interests and questions. Because of this view, Pistoia's administrators have searched to bring into their system teachers and resource personnel who have expertise or preparation from different disciplinary sources—disciplines not only pedagogical and psychological but also social, aesthetic, and anthropological.

Galardini and Giovannini reject the idea of the teacher as an expert technician who has to produce precise results. Instead, the intention is to "reiterate the teacher's original and creative knowledge: whoever has a talent for art, a love of nature, a preference for reading has been encouraged in this direction and considered a precious resource" (Galardini, 2004, p. 22).

Furthermore, they have always encouraged staff members to read seriously and develop a reflective disposition to construct and use specific professional tools for documentation, such as weekly reports (Picchio, Giovannini, Mayer, & Musatti, 2012), the *diario*, or child memory book (Giovannini, 2001), and, in special cases, "notebook for two voices" (between parent and teacher) (e.g., Magrini & Gandini, 2001). They have succeeded in building such a teaching force in Pistoia—partly due to the good insurance, leave, and retirement benefits that make teaching a desirable job, but also due to the strong support systems that enable ongoing professional development. They are able to hire and retain teachers who are eager to become experts, with strong skills of observation, reflection, and documentation.

PRESERVICE EARLY CHILDHOOD TEACHER PREPARATION IN ITALY

Preservice early childhood teacher preparation is the same for Reggio Emilia and Pistoia, indeed for all parts of Italy. The Italian word used for teacher training is *formazione*, based on the same root as the English word "formation," and it conveys the sense of "taking form," as opposed to "being formed" or "being trained" (Nigris, 2007). The emphasis is on developing the internal qualities and interests that teachers bring, rather than imposing expectations about what they need to know and do. Thinking of their preparation as a technical process, such as training for a sport or a skilled craft, would not be correct for Italian teachers.

However, it is only in recent years that this preparation usually takes place at the postsecondary level (Lazzari, Picchio, & Balduzzi, 2015). During most of the decades that the municipal early childhood systems in north and central Italy were being built up, teachers became qualified to be *educatrici* (educators) for preschools and infant-toddler centers through a traditional pathway of attending special secondary schools (*magistrales*), some run by the Catholic Church and others public (OECD, 2006), where they learned the basics of child development, classroom management, room arrangement, leading a lesson, and so on. Therefore, the cities such as Reggio Emilia, Pistoia, Bologna, Genoa, Milan, Modena, Parma, San Miniato, and Trento, with ambitious early childhood administrations, supplemented their teachers' initial preservice training, with thoughtful programs of in-service professional development. As will be described, this learning is a long process where they are immersed in an environment rich with materials and learning exchanges between teachers, children, and families. Their learning will be supported by the other teachers, *atelierista*, and the pedagogical coordinator who meets with all the teachers, cooks, and cleaners once a week in a meeting to discuss the running of the school and to plan together.

Starting as early as the 1980s, however, many educators began to surpass the minimal requirements and attended university programs (Nigris, 2007). In 1998, national legislation established new standards for early childhood teachers. The requirement for preschool teachers became a four-year degree in *Scienze della Formazione Primaria*, a course of study preparing both preschool and primary teachers. In 1999, the Italian university system was reformed in alignment with European agreements, to consist of a three-year level (*laurea*, roughly equivalent to the North American bachelor's degree) and a two-year postgraduate level (*laurea magistrale*, roughly equivalent to the North American master's degree).

Beginning in 2007, the four-year course for preschool teachers was extended to five years, as at all other levels of teacher preparation, which allows them also to compete for elementary school teaching. The trend for infant-toddler teachers in most regions of Italy is to require the three-year course.

The goal of the university programs is to offer multidisciplinary studies with theory and practice integrated and involving a partnership with schools (Nigris, 2007). One such university program is offered by the University of Modena and Reggio Emilia. The new regulations for teacher preparation encourage links between universities, local authorities, and research and training centers, such as the National Research Council (CNR) in Rome, which often cooperates with the early childhood system in Pistoia. Special-needs teachers (teacher assistants) can undertake designated courses, pass relevant entry tests, have an upper secondary school degree, and obtain a two-year specialization as special-needs teachers (OECD, 2006, p. 364).

The reform laws set out general content objectives for university courses in early childhood education in order to develop the teacher's personal identity and competence. They also specify learning objectives in four areas: (1) the self and others; (2) body, movement, and health; (3) receiving and producing messages; and (4) exploring, knowing, and planning (OECD, 2006). Teachers, prepared through the university programs that are offered by several universities in Italian cities, now enter their careers in early childhood much better prepared than in the past when they had only attended secondary school. Nevertheless, in Reggio Emilia and Pistoia, in-service professional development remains a strong priority, to supplement the fundamental professional education received at the university.

IN-SERVICE PROFESSIONAL DEVELOPMENT IN REGGIO EMILIA

From the time the first city schools for young children opened in 1963, Loris Malaguzzi was deeply aware of the need to find a new cultural identity to win trust and respect from parents and the citizens of Reggio Emilia. His strategy in those early years was to build on the experience teachers had gained as part of the cooperative schools started by parents at the end of World War II in 1945 (Gandini, 2012a). Veteran teachers made an essential contribution to the preparation of young teachers.

At the same time, Malaguzzi sought to learn about what was happening in education outside of Italy, in particular in Geneva, Switzerland, where Piaget was active. He also opened up to teachers, parents, and citizens new kinds of learning experiences and conferences, for example, bringing in Gianni Rodari to lecture on fantasy, imagination, and storytelling with children (see Edwards et al., 2014) and David Hawkins, Lilian Katz, and others in 1990 for a conference on the Potentials and Rights of Children (Hawkins, 2012).

This concept of professional development as shared construction among teachers and as public experience with parents and citizens went on to include many cultural initiatives, for instance, taking advantage of scholarly lectures, public theater productions, musical performances, or artistic exhibits that could provide enlightening experiences for adults, or for adults together with children. What started in the early history of the public preschools in Reggio continued on with the same goals, acquiring increasing participation by local educators and eventually reaching out to educators from many parts of the world.

The Induction and Mentoring of New Teachers

The shared construction among teachers begins anew with each new teacher. As a growing system that cherishes innovation, particular and individual attention toward new staff must necessarily occur within each center or school. When a new teacher is hired, she is placed side by side with one of the most seasoned teachers to be "accompanied" and supported in her development. This takes place after the new teacher has completed the preservice course of study at the university and been selected from the official city competition (*concorso*) that combines a written essay prepared by the Pedagogical Coordinating Team with an interview with the team or its director.

In recent years, Reggio Emilia has seen an influx of new teachers, and this has led to some innovations in the process of new teacher induction. Sergio Spaggiari, former director of the Municipal Infant-Toddler Centers and Preschools of Reggio Emilia, reflected on this process in an interview with Lella Gandini (2009). He noted that in some cases, four or five new teachers were placed in an infant-toddler center or preschool, but still there were at least that many experienced teachers there to communicate to them the spirit and messages of the place. At one point, intensive professional development retreats were also organized for new teachers at the beginning of the school year and on other occasions.

The educators in Reggio also undertook an experiment with "tutor" or mentor teachers who provide a situation of reciprocal professional development in various preschools or infant-toddler centers. The mentors move from their home schools into the new situations. They are not expected to behave like little professors or transmit the "true" message;

instead, their role is to encourage and enrich dialogue and the exchange of ideas.

According to Spaggiari, mentoring is a delicate and difficult role and requires a balanced approach between being the one who introduces ideas and the one who responds to them. The mentors bring with them their experiences at their former schools but become open to broadened horizons, realizing that something that they have done in a particular way at their old school can also be done in a different way. This opens up a larger landscape of possibilities for all.

The "Diffuse System" of Professional Development

In general, the process of ongoing professional development for all the teachers continues to evolve in Reggio Emilia due to the increasing complexity of the system of services (Cagliari, Filippini, Giacopini, Bonilauri, & Margini, 2012; Soncini, 2012). There are now three crosscutting or "transversal" *pedagogisti* who coordinate the pedagogical system throughout its entire complexity. These transversals are responsible for the pedagogical coordination within the city of Reggio Emilia and for the professional development of the staff. They are also responsible for collaboration with other educational initiatives in the city and the Emilia Romagna region.

The Reggio administrators have worked closely to conceive and lead a transformation of the professional development system that they call a "diffuse pedagogical system." This "diffuse system" of professional development is not designed for linear, top-down transmission, but instead creates many collegial zones of knowledge creation and exchange. Competences are deepened and enlarged in a forum that ideally promotes learning between older and younger generations, across job categories, and around pedagogical issues of enduring concern.

This new system amplifies tendencies of past years and sharpens earlier emphases, yet also reveals the capacity of the Reggio early childhood system to evolve and adapt to new conditions and challenges. It acts to save what was accumulated through decades of work and could be put at risk by staff turnover, and gives new responsibilities to educators with the deepest roots and expertise.

In their daily discussions and dialogues, teachers and staff offer one another emotional support and encouragement as well as concrete suggestions and advice. In addition, however, a method of extended mutual criticism and self-examination has developed and become accepted. Thus, an important part of ongoing teacher professional development in Reggio Emilia entails a small work group—composed perhaps of teacher(s), mentor teacher, pedagogical coordinator, and *atelierista*—observing and documenting a group of children together, then meeting for lengthy discussion, analysis, and comparison of perspectives. This method of collaborating has been used for many years in Reggio Emilia, with variations according to the annual plans for professional development formulated by the Pedagogical Coordinating Team (Cagliari et al., 2012).

Professional Development through Formal Reflective Discussion

Another powerful initiative that created continual professional development emerged from the creation and increasing complexity of the exhibit that opened in Reggio Emilia in 1981 with the title *When the Eye Jumps over the Wall* and then took the name *The Hundred Languages of Children* when it landed in the United States in 1987. The exhibit has been a constant tool of professional development for the educators of Reggio Emilia, and the authors of this chapter have analyzed its inspiration and power (Edwards, Gandini, & Forman, 2012, pp. 11–13). Several different versions of the exhibit have been on tour around the world.

It is necessary to consider the learning impact that producing and renovating the exhibit has had on the educators of Reggio Emilia, because the selection of images and creation of text for each theme involves the teachers who did the particular work with children. As of 2015, the educators from Reggio Emilia report that about four thousand educators have been visiting the schools in Reggio Emilia in each of the last few years, and thousands more have attended conferences in their own countries.

Educators from Reggio Emilia (teachers, *atelieristi*, and pedagogical coordinators) have traveled for other presentations, often on the occasion of conferences associated with the exhibit in northern Europe, North and South America, Asia, Africa, and Australia. These presentations contribute many moments of professional development to the speakers as they plan their topics, select stories and images to show, respond to audience questions, and interact with diverse groups. When teachers go from a simple documentation to preparing a complex panel or slideshow with photographs and captions that explain a sequence of learning events, they must bring to bear all of their intellectual, artistic, and communicative artistic talents.

Indeed, focusing on the study groups visiting Reggio Emilia, it is evident that the ongoing cycle of organized visits to the infant-toddler centers and preschools creates the final and most distinctive piece of the process of in-service professional development. All of the centers and schools are systematically involved, since articulating what they are about is considered formative for staff as much as visitors.

In such a school or center visit, a typical routine is followed. The group of visitors (perhaps thirty in number) first gathers in a quiet room to receive a brief history and introduction to the context delivered by one or two teachers and an *atelierista* and/or pedagogical coordinator. Then, visitors fan out to observe and make their own notes and observations for an hour or so. Finally, visitors gather again for another extended period to share observations and reactions and ask questions of the hosts, for example, about work in the *atelier*, use of unusual tools and recycled materials, innovations in gardening and cooking with families, the incorporation of immigrant children, or inclusion of children with special needs. The preparation, carrying out, and later debriefing of the session provides a boost to the hosts' morale and the source of new insight into what they are doing, and why.

IN-SERVICE PROFESSIONAL DEVELOPMENT IN PISTOIA

Continuous professional development for everyone from beginning teachers to experienced veterans is a key feature of professional support in Pistoia, in some similar and some contrasting strategies to Reggio Emilia. This support begins with the coherent design of the overall educational project and an effective coordinating team, but is implemented through the promotion of collegiality within infant-toddler centers, preschools, and laboratories, with close mentoring of new teachers. In addition, an annual program of in-service courses and meetings is carefully planned, and collaboration is promoted with research agencies in Italy, Europe, and the United States (Becchi, 2010; Picchio et al., 2012; for the case of Parma, see Terzi & Cantarelli, 2001).

The Promotion of Collegiality within "Collectives" (Groups) of Teachers

Pistoia first of all depends on a wide interpretation of educational work to provide continual educational mentoring and renewal of teachers. Mentorship of new teachers is critical, and each beginner is paired with an experienced teacher for close mentoring to take place in the class-room. Furthermore, teacher turnover is low and groups of teachers customarily remain together as stable collectives over time, allowing for them to make gradual changes and improvements in their settings. Each context—infant-toddler center, preschool, or special laboratory—is encouraged to seek its own identity and draw on all possible resources to permit the adults (educators and family members) to find ways to express their particular talents and interests in aesthetic or cultural areas that might be enriching (see Cline et al., 2012; Edwards et al., 2014).

This inclusive embrace of individual contributions promotes person-al and common growth "because it enriches and gratifies those who experience or take part in it . . . adults and children alike use new capacities" (Galardini, 2004, p. 22). Indeed, these considerations were the springboard for the special laboratories (*Area Bambini*) and part-time programs for parents and very young children that also serve as sites for teacher training in skills such as technology, oral traditions, puppetry, and connections with immigrant families coming from over-seas (portrayed in the DVD *Bambini: Infant-Toddler Care in Pistoia; A Child-Friendly City,* Great Plains National Inc., 2002).

When Donatella Giovannini was asked "How do the teachers stay rich and lively in their teaching, without becoming monotonous?" she talked about the continual local innovation, or problem solving and experimentation, in providing experiences, activities, and environments for young children. This is not a matter of each teacher heading off in his or her own random direction, but rather of the collective discussing and deciding together, often with the involvement of the pedagogical coordinator:

This is an aspect of my work that is very difficult because it is very easy for educative work to become limp, lose its significance, and become routine. We are challenged day after day to keep today's events different from yesterdays. One of my jobs is to encourage teachers and to coordinate our various activities. Teachers' ideas for new events are brought to me, and as a group, we discuss benefits and improvements to those ideas, (Giovannini, interview, 2001)

The Formal Program of Professional Development

To supplement the everyday mentoring and coaching, the annual program of in-service professional meetings has maintained a tradition of distinguished quality for many years. This program was initiated under the leadership of Annalia Galardini and run by the pedagogical coordinating team in the Office of Public Instruction for the municipality. All of the educators from the infant-toddler and preschool system are invited and expected to participate, and the courses are well attended.

The program consists of one-time lectures and workshops as well as short courses that continue to meet on several scheduled occasions. The lecturers or session facilitators are typically drawn from Italian universities (e.g., faculty who have published in the field, from Universities of Florence, Pavia, and Rome); the National Research Council (CNR) in Rome; and the Regional Administration of Tuscany. Often, certain faculty return year after year with new material, which reduces the impersonality of the sessions and increases their effectiveness through familiarity and shared meaning.

In addition, the initiative brings in noted artists, writers, and other cultural leaders from the locality or even abroad (e.g., Eric Carle, famous children's book author and illustrator from Northampton, Massachusetts, visited in 2005 as part of an extended project with Pistoia and the University of Florence; see Edwards et al., 2014). Further, workshops or book discussion groups may be led by educators from within the Pistoia early childhood system who have particular expertise.

Loris Malaguzzi and Vea Vecchi from Reggio Emilia and the authors of this chapter are among those who have led meetings as part of this annual program. The meetings are formal, serious, and scholarly, yet festive, lively, highly interactive, and suffused with the pleasure of long-term relationships taking place in a setting that invites questioning on particular points but confirms trust in overall direction and progress.

Topics of meetings in two recent years have included:

- Continuity in services for children birth to age six
- Connections between preschool and primary
- Explorations of nature and natural materials with children
- Immigrant families in Pistoia and children growing up bilingual
- Improving practice for children with special needs
- Construction of toys, storytelling, and preparing food with children after school

In other years, topics were equally far ranging, including, for example:

- Pedagogical observation and documentation
- *Inserimento*, or the process of settling new children and families into infant-toddler classrooms
- Anthropology and education
- The child in history (1800–1900)
- Emerging literacy
- Block play
- Bedtime as a moment of attachment stress
- Montessori's legacy
- Implications of changing family and racial demographics

The purpose is for participants to deepen their insights into big ideas and reflective educational practice, rather than to acquire technical or procedural knowledge and skills. Donatella Giovannini, who has long been involved in a leadership role in organizing professional development, says, "This profession is not something one learns all at once; instead, one must mature with the profession." In her view, since teaching conditions transform so rapidly—they are so different today from twenty or thirty years ago—it is critical to get *innovation* into what teachers are doing. "Innovation gives teachers a sense that their work is important. I think good teachers must be articulate and proud, not only of their work but also socially and culturally" (Giovannini, personal communication, 2015).

Collaborations with Research Agencies

Educational renewal and innovation are pursued in Pistoia through the promotion of teachers' critical reflection on everyday practices "rather than through the transmission of theoretical knowledge or training of discrete skills" (Lazzari, Picchio, & Musatti, 2013, p. 13). These outcomes have been fostered not only by everyday coaching and the formal program of professional development, but also by close cooperation with research agencies.

To supplement internal resources, educators in Pistoia have partnered with external researchers to pursue scientific investigations through teacher action-research. The authors of this chapter (sponsored by the Universities of Massachusetts, Amherst, and Kentucky) have engaged in several research partnerships in Pistoia to study parents' and teachers' expectations for children's developmental timetables; cooperation and community among children; and from 1995 to 1999, a study of the growth of relationships ("attachments") between parents and educators of children under age three (Edwards & Gandini, 2001).

At the end of that third study on the growth of relationships, Donatella Giovannini was interviewed about what effects, if any, she thought participation in the research had on the study teachers. These teachers had already proved critical to the research in terms of recruiting parents, taking videotapes at the beginning of each year of children's adjustment, sharing their documentations, and facilitating researcher-parent interviews.

Giovannini saw several types of benefits for teachers of becoming partners in the research study. For example, it was positive for teachers to be part of a working group with colleagues from other infant-toddler centers. Because of the duration and continuity of the research, the relationships among the teachers (within and between the different centers) became more consolidated.

Teachers also became more aware of and articulate about the strategies for building relationships with families. They had used these before but now found them to be more apparent and meaningful. In addition, teachers were able to improve and consolidate their close relationships with particular children and parents; they became more aware of these developing relationships through the reflective processes involved in the research methods.

Through these processes, they became more aware of and more competent with regard to strategies of documentation. They found that the requirements and deadlines built into systematic data collection increased their capacity for a certain kind of responsibility. And finally, teachers gained confidence from seeing their administrative leaders (and the researchers) investing time, attention, energy, and ideas in them (Edwards & Gandini, 2001).

In recent years, Pistoia has participated in an even longer term and more significant research partnership with researchers from the National Research Council in Rome (Lazzari, Picchio, & Musatti, 2013; Musatti, Picchio, & Mayer, 2011; Picchio et al., 2012; Picchio, Di Giandomenico, & Musatti, 2014). This project is focused on finding new ways for teachers to improve their reflective capacities through documentation and analysis of children's experiences. Experimentation was conducted on teachers' use of weekly journals to prepare overall summaries of long-term learning. In this way, they learned to describe events occurring in a given setting, and identified the relations linking them together in order to grasp their meanings. They analyzed in terms of home-school transitions, social processes, children's activities, routine care moments, use of space, and use of time (Picchio, Di Giandomenico, & Musatti, 2014).

This research project, like the one with Edwards and Gandini, involved a "co-learning partnership" (rather than purely a "data extraction" research model) that reflected the preferred style that Pistoia administrators interact with their staff, the public, and outside visitors, and in turn by teachers with their colleagues and families. The educational system in Pistoia benefits from being small enough that its leadership allows a personalized ("empathy-based") rather than bureaucratic mode of operation. The system has been stable over time and coherent in its principles, yet also seeking to be resourceful, open to change, and dynamic in its forward movement.

CONCLUSION

This chapter began by describing the myth of Ariadne offering thread to find the way through the maze's complications as a metaphor for the role of teachers in Reggio Emilia who give orientation, meaning, and value to the experience of the schools. Teachers are the ones who hold the threads to construct and interweave the connections and relationships and transform them into meaningful communications and learning.

Pedagogical documentation—giving visibility to the pathways traced in teaching and learning through analysis of images, notes, and interpretations—is the fundamental procedure that sustains the educational action and the dialogue of teachers together with children. This process serves as the central tool for in-service development in Reggio Emilia, used in new teacher induction, within-school dialogue, and study tours to the preschools and infant-toddler centers.

This Reggio approach contrasts with the focus on "empathic teaching" in Pistoia. There, trust and respect emanating from the director and pedagogical coordinators provide space for creativity within each center and preschool, so that teachers, staff, and families are able to elaborate over time their own distinctive style of teamwork and strategies for implementing the system's mission and goals. Teachers mentor one another, coconstruct their particular cultural interests and strengths, and execute overarching goals in their own way in close-knit teams, always supported by the pedagogical coordinators.

Schools and families also access special laboratories (*Area Bambini*) to learn alongside expert teachers and enrich their skills in such fields as nature exploration, storytelling, toy making, and the arts. Researchers from outside agencies and universities meet with teachers from all the schools in the formal annual program of professional development, or visit the schools and engage in conversations as partners in research, leading to innovations and improvement.

In both Reggio and Pistoia, reflection, dialogue, and preference for slow, careful, incremental improvements in educational philosophy and practice are the established norm. Reggio Emilia and Pistoia provide two complementary visions of how this is possible. In both cases, learning is a long process, individualized to the individuals' level of initial preservice preparation, responsive to their particular talents and interests, but most importantly immersing them in in-service experiences of mentoring and peer relations, where they construct teaching knowledge through cyclical processes of modeling, observation, experimentation, interdisciplinary study, formal trainings, and critical reflection with others.

REFERENCES

Becchi, E. (2010). *Una pedagogia del buon gusto: Experienze e progetti nei servizi educativi per l'infanzia del Comune di Pistoia*. [Pedagogy of "good taste": Experiences and projects in Pistoia municipal ECE services]. Milan, Italy: FrancoAngeli.

Cagliari, P., Filippini, T., Giacopini, E., Bonilauri, S., & Margini, D. (2012). The Pedagogical Coordinating Team and professional development. In C. P. Edwards, L. Gandini, & G. Forman (Eds.), *The hundred languages of children: The Reggio Emilia experience in transformation* (3rd ed., pp. 135–146). Santa Barbara, CA: Praeger.

Cline, K. D., Edwards, C. P., Gandini, L., Giacomelli, A., Giovannini, D., & Galardini, A. (2012). A day at Filastrocca Preschool, Pistoia, Italy: Meaning making through literacy and creative activity. *LEARNing Landscapes, 6*(1), 107–128. http://digitalcommons.unl.edu/famconfacpub/83/

Edwards, C. P., Cline, K. D., Gandini, L., Giacomelli, A., Giovannini, D., & Galardini, A. (2014). Books, stories, and the imagination at "The Nursery Rhyme": A qualitative case study of a preschool learning environment in Pistoia, Italy. *Journal of Research in Childhood Education, 28*, 1–25. http://digitalcommons.unl.edu/famconfacpub/106/

Edwards, C. P., & Gandini, L. (2001). Research as a partnership for learning together: Studying the growth of relationships inside the *nido*. In L. Gandini & C. P. Edwards (Eds.), *Bambini: The Italian approach to infant/toddler care* (pp. 181–199). New York, NY: Teachers College Press.

Edwards, C. P., & Gandini, L. (2015). Teacher research in Reggio Emilia, Italy: Essence of a dynamic, evolving role. *Voices of Practitioners: Teacher Research in Early Childhood Education, 10*(1), 89–103. http://naeyc.org/files/naeyc/Teacher%20Research%20in%20Reggio%20Emilia.pdf

Edwards, C. P., Gandini, L., & Forman, G. (Eds.) (1993). *The hundred languages of children: The Reggio Emilia approach to early childhood education*. Norwood, NJ: Ablex.

Edwards, C. P., Gandini, L., & Forman, G. (Eds.). (2012). *The hundred languages of children: The Reggio Emilia experience in transformation* (3rd ed.). Santa Barbara, CA: Praeger.

Edwards, C. P., Gandini, L., & Nimmo, J. (2015). *Loris Malaguzzi and the teachers: Dialogues on collaboration and conflict, Reggio Emilia, 1990*. Lincoln: University of Nebraska Libraries, Zea Books. http://digitalcommons.unl.edu/zeabook/29/

Fortunati, A. (2007). Italy: Quality. In R. S. New & M. Cochran (Eds.), *Early childhood education: An international encyclopedia* (Vol. 4, pp. 1122–1125). Westport, CT: Praeger.

Galardini, A. (2004). Cultivating quality. In *Education in Pistoia* (pp. 18–22). Bergamo, Italy: Edizioni Junior.

Galardini, A., & Giovannini, D. (2001). Pistoia: Creating a dynamic, open system to serve children, families, and community. In L. Gandini & C. P. Edwards (Eds.), *Bambini: The Italian approach to infant/toddler care* (pp. 89–108). New York, NY: Teachers College Press.

Gandini, L. (2009). Renewal and regeneration of an educational community: An interview with Sergio Spaggiari. *Innovations in Early Education: The International Reggio Exchange, 16*(2), 1–6.

Gandini, L. (2012a). History, ideas, and basic principles: An interview with Loris Malaguzzi. In C. P. Edwards, L. Gandini, & G. Forman (Eds.), *The hundred languages of children: The Reggio Emilia experience in transformation* (3rd ed., pp. 27–72). Santa Barbara, CA: Praeger.

Gandini, L. (2012b). The *atelier*: A conversation with Vea Vecchi. In C. P. Edwards, L. Gandini, & G. Forman (Eds.), *The hundred languages of children: The Reggio Emilia experience in transformation* (3rd ed., pp. 302–316). Santa Barbara, CA: Praeger.

Gandini, L., & Edwards, C. P. (Eds.). (2001). *Bambini: The Italian approach to infant/toddler care*. New York, NY: Teachers College Press.

Giovannini, D. (2001). Traces of childhood: A child's diary. In L. Gandini & C. P. Edwards (Eds.), *Bambini: The Italian approach to infant/toddler care* (pp. 146–151). New York, NY: Teachers College Press.

Great Plains National Inc. (2002, November). *Bambini: Infant-Toddler Care in Pistoia; A Child-Friendly City*. DVD. Available from Child Development Media Inc. www. childdevelopmentmedia.com

Hawkins, D. (2012). Malaguzzi's story, other stories, and respect for children. In C. P. Edwards, L. Gandini, & G. Forman (Eds.), *The hundred languages of children: The Reggio Emilia experience in transformation* (3rd ed., pp. 73–80). Santa Barbara, CA: Praeger.

Lazzari, A., Picchio, M., & Balduzzi, L. (2015). Professionalisation policies in the ECEC field: Trends and tensions in the Italian context. *International Journal of Early Years Education, 23*(3), 274–287.

Lazzari, A., Picchio, M., & Musatti, T. (2013). Sustaining ECEC quality through continuing professional development: Systemic approaches to practitioners' professionalization in the Italian context. *Early Years: An International Research Journal, 33*(2), 133–145.

Magrini, G., & Gandini, L. (2001). Inclusion: Dario's story. In L. Gandini & C. P. Edwards (Eds.), *Bambini: The Italian approach to infant/toddler care* (pp. 152–163). New York, NY: Teachers College Press.

Mantovani, S. (Ed.). (1998). Incontri, confronti, dissensi, nostalgie. In S. Mantovani (Ed.), *Nostalgia del futuro: Liberare speranze per una nuova cultura dell'infanzia* [Nostalgia for the future: Unleashing hope for a new culture of childhood] (pp. 3–10). Bergamo, Italy: Edizioni Junior.

Musatti, T., Picchio, M., & Mayer, S. (2011). *A continuous support to professionalism: The case of Pistoia ECE provision. European Commission: Report prepared for the CoRe project.* Brussels, Belgium.

Nigris, E. (2007). Italy: Teacher training. In R. S. New & M. Cochran (Eds.), *Early childhood education: An international encyclopedia* (Vol. 4, pp. 1145–1150). Westport, CT: Praeger.

OECD (Organization for Economic Co-operation and Development). (2006). *Starting strong II: Early childhood education and care*. Paris, France: OECD.

Picchio, M., Di Giandomenico, I., & Musatti, T. (2014). The use of documentation in a participatory system of evaluation. *Early Years: An International Research Journal, 34*(2), 133–145.

Picchio, M., Giovannini, D., Mayer, S., & Musatti, T. (2012). Documentation and analysis of children's experience: An ongoing collegial activity for early childhood professionals. *Early Years: An International Research Journal, 32*(2), 159–170.

Rinaldi, C. (1998). *Malaguzzi e le insegnanti* [Malaguzzi and the teachers]. In S. Mantovani (Ed.), *Nostalgia del futuro: Liberare speranze per una nuova cultura dell'infanzia* [Nostalgia for the future: Unleashing hope for a new culture of childhood] (pp. 197–200). Bergamo, Italy: Edizioni Junior.

Soncini, I. (2012). The inclusive community. In C. P. Edwards, L. Gandini, & G. Forman (Eds.), *The hundred languages of children: The Reggio Emilia experience in transformation* (3rd ed., pp. 187–212). Santa Barbara, CA: Praeger.

Terzi, N., & Cantarelli, M. (2001). Parma: Supporting the work of teachers through professional development, organization, and administrative support. In L. Gandini & C. P. Edwards (Eds.), *Bambini: The Italian approach to infant/toddler care* (pp. 78–88). New York, NY: Teachers College Press.

5

INTEGRATING WALDORF EDUCATION PRINCIPLES WITH TRADITIONAL TEACHER EDUCATION

Gilad Goldshmidt

Lior, twenty-three years old, wanted to be an elementary school teacher. She wanted to help young children achieve a different, nurturing, constructive, and encouraging school experience, different from what she herself had experienced. Her searches led her to the Waldorf education studies at the David Yellin College of Education in Jerusalem, a program that would give her the professional education she sought and a B.A. The degree was the key to working in states schools supervised by the Ministry of Education, where working conditions include social benefits.

Toward the end of her first year, Lior was beginning to have her doubts. Her initial enthusiasm and resolve had all but deserted her. She was overwhelmed by the difficulty of combining Waldorf education studies with academic studies:

> On the one hand, they want me to be a researcher, to read articles, summarize, analyze, critique, and judge, while on the other they want me to sing, play an instrument, dance, paint, and sculpt. Here they want me to bring everything to a point, an answer, an unequivocal statement; there they want philosophical discussions, in-depth conversations, and mutual listening. On the academic side I've got a huge workload, I always have to prepare, sit exams, revise. On the Waldorf side everything is a process, there's time and space.

According to Lior, the teachers in both programs are good and she greatly appreciates them. However, she says, "This is about two completely different tunes and I don't know how I can combine them."

To examine the relationships and challenges of training that combines Waldorf education with academic studies I shall attempt to describe them from several perspectives: the philosophy underlying this educational approach, the characteristics of the training itself, the characteristics of the students who undergo the training, and the complex relationship between the college's academic aspect and the Waldorf program.

THE PRINCIPLES OF WALDORF EDUCATION

The educational approach known as "Waldorf education" or "Steiner education" has flourished in Israel in recent years. At the time of writing, spring 2016, there are more than one hundred kindergartens, twenty-one elementary schools, five high schools, and six teacher education institutions working in the spirit of Waldorf education nationwide.[1]

Waldorf education is primarily based on the books, lectures, and studies of Rudolf Steiner, founder of this educational approach. Already in his lifetime, Steiner's approach became a large educational movement that included Waldorf schools in various cities in Germany, Switzerland, England, and the United States (Dietrich, 2006). At present, the Waldorf education movement is considered to be the largest independent school movement in the world (Zander, 2007). Its educational method can be characterized by the following principles:

Applying Developmental Thinking

Waldorf education is based upon developmental psychology derived from the spiritual studies of Rudolf Steiner (Steiner, 1965). Underlying it is a division of childhood into three six- to seven-year periods (birth to 6–7 years, 6–7 to 13–14, 13–14 to 20–21), with educational efforts in each period focused on nurturing different qualities. In the first—activity, senses, play, and movement; art and aesthetics and storytelling in the second; and abstract thinking, handwork in workshops and various crafts, and community involvement in the third (Edmunds, 2004; Steiner, 1965).

However, developmental thinking does not end there; it permeates the entire educational practice in Waldorf schools. Thus, for example, the curricula and teaching methods are adapted to the chronological age and characteristics of each and every class—the way the pupils are accompanied and the discourse with them vary in accordance with their age, and even art teaching places emphasis on different forms at each and every age (Richter, 2006).

A Holistic View of the Child and Educational Processes

In his educational writings, Steiner repeatedly wrote about education and teaching from within the whole person (Steiner, 1983). This is a holistic, multifaceted view of teaching processes, education, and the accompaniment of children.

This holistic view is manifested in numerous characteristics of Waldorf schools (Easton, 1997), for example, in the balance between theoretical, artistic, and physical spheres in the teaching schedule. Accordingly, each child can experience handwork, artistic creation, and theoretical study in the course of every school day. As a result, by the end of their schooling each child has experienced all the fields of learning and is educated through many and varied fields of endeavor and learning, without electives and without specialization.

The Importance of the Artistic Experience in the Teaching Process

The phrase "the art of education" recurs in Steiner's educational lectures and writings, as he addressed the crucial role of art and artistic processes in the school. Steiner (1978) wrote about the ability of art to empower and nurture emotions, its ability to reinforce willpower and practice (1977), its balancing and curative influence, and its latent potential as a methodic means (1983).

Waldorf schools employ art as one of the most significant tools in positioning art as an important field of study in its own right, in using artistic means as a significant methodic tool in each and every field, and as an aesthetic approach to the school setting (Edmunds, 2004; Steiner, 1965).

Joint Administration: A Republic of Teachers

In his opening address at the first teacher training course he held in the newly established first school, Steiner (1980) emphasized that he intended to establish a school founded on joint administration. Since then, in numerous schools worldwide, the Waldorf education movement has accorded center place to this ideal of a "republican administration." While the ideal is expressed differently in each country, it can be found in virtually every anthroposophy-inspired educational practice (Leber, 1991). I shall demonstrate how this is manifested in teacher training later in this chapter.

TEACHER TRAINING IN THE SPIRIT OF WALDORF EDUCATION

Teacher training in the spirit of Waldorf education was also born of the principles noted above (Barz, 2013; Gabert, 1961). The four-year training program incorporates the following training characteristics:

Emphasis on Inner Development

The question of the developing person is central in teacher training: "Everything hinges on developing the emotions" (Steiner, 2010, p. 31), beginning with emphasis on developing the educator's personality. The Waldorf approach is, that when teachers stand before their pupils, first and foremost they bring themselves, their personality, and their inner skills, all of which influence the children more than anything else.

Krishnamurti (1987), who in many respects was connected to Steiner, wrote, "Thus education, in the true sense, is the understanding of oneself, for it is within each one of us that the whole of existence is gathered" (p. 14). How, then, can we pave the way for students of education to develop inner strengths? How can they embark on a path of inner development? The following are a few examples:

Self-contemplation and self-knowledge are practiced in the first year as part of a course devoted to human biography. The study of biography was researched in depth by Steiner and his successors, and is currently used in numerous places as an anthroposophy-inspired therapy tool (Lievegoed, 2003).

In this course, the students, under the close supervision of a skilled instructor, present their life story to the group, as a means for the student to attain self-knowledge and work on various psychological elements. In the subsequent years the students continue engaging with biographical questions while delving into myths and legends that constitute a sort of archetypical life story (Campbell, 2008) in which each of us can find his or her place.

A course on the teacher's inner path is usually added in the second or third year of training, and includes contemplation and meditation techniques, in addition to concentration exercises, all of which are part of the anthroposophical corpus of knowledge (Steiner, 1947, 1972).

One such contemplation exercise is done in the evening. The students try to see themselves, without judgment, as if from a high observation point, from the end of the day back to the start (Steiner, 1947). The students do the exercise at home every day and share their experiences in class, consult, and help one another under the teacher's guidance.

At this point it is important to note that every spiritual-meditative exercise in an anthroposophical setting, and all the more so in teacher training, is given to the judgment and decision of the individual. As freedom and autonomy are the first principle of the anthroposophical approach (Steiner, 1964), everything in the training takes the form of a recommendation and is optional.

A graduate group art project is held at the end of the third year and provides another excellent opportunity for inner developmental work. The project is led by the students themselves with guidance and assistance provided by some of their teachers. While the actual outcome—a presentation for fellow students, teachers, friends, and family—the work process is no less important. The work process presents motifs for observing the social relationships between the members of the group, and helps develop inner strengths, inner authority, independent thinking, and creative powers.

Developing Artistic Skills

Earlier we noted the importance of art in Waldorf schools. Clearly, teachers in this educational approach must possess sharp artistic senses and work on them as much as possible. First and foremost, they must be "artists in education and teaching" (Gabert, 1961, p. 167).

This element of the teacher as an artist is manifested in the teacher training in intensive artistic work in a wide range of arts throughout all the years of training. The artistic fields occupy at least one-third of all teacher training hours (Barz, 2013; Gabert, 1961), and include music, poetry, sculpture, drawing and painting, drama, eurythmy (an expressive movement art originated by Steiner [1984]), and their combinations.

These arts serve to develop and nurture the artistic senses, sensitivity, a sense of balance and harmony, contemplation ability, self-knowledge, and many additional gifts that artistic endeavor can bestow (Eisner, 2002). It is important to note that this is not about professional artistic training to become a painter, a musician, or a sculptor, but rather development of the inner senses on which the teacher builds work in a Waldorf school (Gabert, 1961).

Reading and Studying Anthroposophic Writings

Steiner used the German term *Menschenkunde* (the study of man) to describe the spiritual and psychological philosophy underlying Waldorf education, and repeatedly encouraged his teachers to study, delve into, and think about this "study of man." He saw a clear essential and ideological connection between the spiritual-conceptual content into which the teacher delves and thinks about and the educational practice, and he tried to reinforce and encourage this connection.

At one of the teacher training courses he taught, Steiner (1983) told his students that the observations proposed by anthroposophical pedagogy "have as their aim a more intimate knowledge of the human being. When you meditate on them, you cannot halt their continued effect within yourself" (p. 51).

This, of course, is given significant expression in teacher training, where emphasis is placed on in-depth study of the writings of Steiner and his successors (see, for example, Richter, 2006), and on an attempt to draw spiritual inspiration from them for each and every detail of the educational practice. Learning is spiral, so that in the first year they learn the foundations of the anthroposophical approach (Steiner, 2008), and in the following years they go on to more detailed and advanced writings.

The method of learning is no less important than the content. Emphasis is placed on active, dialogical study, often in pairs or small groups, combined with writing papers and projects, all of which are directed at the inner aspect of the learning process.

Mentoring toward Observation of Children

One of the skills expected from a teacher at a Waldorf school is the ability to observe children and "read" them: to understand their requests and needs, to hear what they would want to say if they were able to speak from the inner center of their being (Gabert, 1961). Consequently, observation of the children is a salient point of teacher training in the spirit of Waldorf education. As part of the various courses, and each year anew in slightly different form, the students are required to observe children of different ages and record and study their observations. Among the foci of observations are:

- The child's physical-external appearance: size, height, body proportions, skin, hair, and eye color, dress, and so forth
- The child's movement: how he or she sits, stands, walks, runs, and so forth
- Psychological qualities such as expressing emotions and inner experiences
- The cognitive and learning aspect: learning abilities, talents, learning disabilities
- The child's social behavior

It is important to note that the observations are not about judgment, expressing an opinion, or classification and categorization. Rather, they are pure observations employing a Goethean method (Bortoft, 1996), which serves for the inner deepening of the observer and creating an inner impression of the child in order to better understand him or her.

Work on observation of children continues beyond teacher training and constitutes one of the fields of study and practice for the teaching staff in Waldorf schools. This work is methodically practiced at staff meetings and serves as a method for learning about children, classes, educational problems, and challenges associated with children in school (Wiechert, 2012).

Developing Listening, Discourse, and Social Skills

As we have seen, Waldorf schools are jointly administered by a teacher team that usually includes all the educators working there (Leber, 1991; Steiner, 1980). This type of administration, in which there is no hierarchy, in which every teacher is also an administrator, and thus discourse and mutual understanding are at the center of the administration processes, requires mentoring in the course of teacher training and, of course, in the school itself (Rawson, 2010).

Among other things, this refers to the development of abilities such as listening, conversation skills, sensitivity to the other, teamwork, and self-knowledge. Work and practice on these abilities is manifested in teacher training in the following spheres:

- In theoretical lessons greater emphasis is placed on conversation and circle work rather than on frontal lectures. There is work on texts in groups or pairs, and various group assignments. Many lessons are directed toward theoretical projects undertaken by groups of students, which require practice of the abovementioned abilities.
- Art lessons are directed toward expression in plays, exhibitions, or a combination of different art forms around a particular theme. In these projects the students are required to work intensively as a team in many and varied spheres of art and handwork.
- Students learn the principles of joint administration in the work of a Waldorf school and practice them in small assignments associated with teacher training.

STUDENTS, ADMISSION TO THE PROGRAM, EVALUATION, AND FEEDBACK

The students at David Yellin College of Education in Jerusalem come from a variety of backgrounds: women and men, religious and secular, Jews and Arabs (and among the Arab students there are both Muslims and Christians); they come from all parts of Israel and are of different ages (with the majority in their twenties). Therefore, from a human standpoint the group is very varied. Every year fifty to sixty students begin their training in the Waldorf training, with some 80 percent completing it.

The vast majority of students come to the college especially for Waldorf training. In many cases they are young people in their twenties who find an answer to their spiritual search in Waldorf training. A large number of students have had spiritual experiences of one kind or another, and spiritual questions, concepts, and practices are not new to them.

Students connected to Jewish tradition and various forms of Jewish religion will seek to enrich their Jewish-religious worldview and subsequently Jewish-traditional education from perspectives, values, and methods drawn from the world of Waldorf education. Similarly, some of the Muslim and/or Christian students internalize and learn Waldorf education principles and methods and adapt them to their schools and communities of origin.

Admission to the program follows the general conditions for the college, with the addition of a personal interview with the heads of the program. In the interview we ascertain the candidates' motivation to study in the program, review their personal background, answer questions, clarify their connection with education and teaching, and try to verify their suitability for study in the Waldorf program.

Evaluation and feedback processes in the Waldorf program combine the accepted evaluation at the college with specific Waldorf evaluation. The former are primarily based on examinations and papers that are evaluated numerically, and the latter include the following elements:

- A periodic personal conversation with the group's pedagogical counselor whose role is to hold a dialogue with the students about

their progress, and help them through personal crises throughout
their training
- Group discussions—moderated by the group's counselor—on various subjects associated both with the personal and developmental
aspects of each student, as well as the group aspect
- Art project—personal work such as composing a song or musical
piece, writing a story or a poem, sculpture, painting and drawing,
as well as group projects such as a play, an exhibit, choral singing,
and so forth
- Monitoring the students' work in the field starting from the second year

A full listing of all program courses appears in table 5.1.

TEACHER TRAINING IN THE SPIRIT OF WALDORF EDUCATION AND ACADEME

The connection between Waldorf education and the academic world is
not self-evident, and in most countries there is virtually no discourse
and substantive connection between them (Volker, 2012). Whereas in
some European countries Waldorf teacher training has gained recognition as an independent academic institution, the combination of training in the spirit of Waldorf education within an academic institution is,
to the best of my knowledge, extremely rare and currently exists only in
Vienna.[2]

Hence the Waldorf Education Program at David Yellin College of
Education in Jerusalem, which provides full, recognized training and
certification to work in Waldorf schools, is unique not only in Israel, but
in the international context as well.

Going back to Lior's story, we recall that at the end of her first year
in the Waldorf program, she found it difficult to combine the requirements and qualities of academic training and those of the Waldorf program. Indeed, this double set of requirements and qualities poses considerable difficulties and challenges for many teachers and students
alike. To examine this challenge, I shall now present the commonalities
of the two approaches and what distinguishes each of them.

Table 5.1.   Waldorf Education Syllabus at David Yellin College of Education in Jerusalem

	Year 1	Year 2	Year 3	Year 4	Total
(a) Training: Theoretical and general education studies					
Philosophy of education	1	1	1	1	4
Sociology of education	1	1			2
Teaching methods and integration of children with special needs into a heterogeneous class			1	1	2
Art as an educational and methodic tool in a Waldorf school	1	1	1	1	4
Teaching the discipline		2			2
Qualitative research approaches in education	1				1
Quantitative research	1				1
Educational research				2	2
Practical experience in Waldorf schools	1	2	3		6
Practical disciplinary experience (in a field of knowledge chosen by the student)		3	3		6
Total					**30**
(b) Specialization studies					
Main specialization (the field of knowledge the student chooses to expand—Bible, language, history, literature, etc.)	8	8	8	2	26
Total					**26**
Studies in the spirit of Waldorf education					
Rudolf Steiner's educational-developmental approach	2	2	2	2	8

Myths and legends and their role in Waldorf education		2			2
The perception of the evolution of human consciousness as a basis for Waldorf education			2		2
Biography and human development studies	2				2
Jewish festivals and the Jewish calendar				1	1
Total					**15**

Interdisciplinary studies: Art as shaping human development

Movement and eurythmy	1	1	1	1	4
Drama, speech formation, and theater	1	1	1		3
Music, singing, and recorder	1	1	1		3
Sculpture, painting, and drawing	1	1	1		3
Handicrafts as a formative tool		1	1		2
Total					**15**

Foundation and enrichment studies

Hebrew language	2				2
English proficiency for reading academic text	2				2
Computer literacy		1			1
Israeli (Jewish) culture				1	1
Civics and democracy			1		1
Diversity and variety in Israeli society		1			1
Israeli society (Waldorf)	1				1
Total					**9**

Security and safety	1				1
First aid				1	1

Road safety	I	I
Total degree hours		**98**

Waldorf Education and the Academic World: Commonalities

Both approaches emphasize the students' in-depth study of central issues in the philosophy of education, educational thought, and the history and sociology of education. The students' exposure to educational ideas, educational issues, and philosophical dilemmas provides the future teachers with a perspective, expands their knowledge, and can nurture a humanistic and value-oriented mind-set, a mind-set that in the view of many scholars is important for teaching and educating (Aloni, 2007).

In addition, both approaches place considerable emphasis on the students' fieldwork and on monitored classroom work, as well as to the social aspect and to group and class work. Similar to other teacher training colleges in Israel, at David Yellin College of Education, the students study in one core group (unlike university studies), and studies are attended by various social processes.

Waldorf training and academic teacher education both accompany the students in their learning and teaching processes and in their practical experience in the field. In teacher education colleges in Israel it is customary to work in a relatively small group of twenty to thirty students, accompanied by a pedagogic counselor. In many cases this is not only purely professional guidance but also personal guidance that includes the students; personal life and endeavors to see them as developing human beings in as many spheres as possible.

Waldorf Education and the Academic World: Differences

Whereas in teacher training in the spirit of Waldorf education emphasis is placed on the student's inner developmental and even personal aspects, in academic training it is placed on the scientific aspect, on accumulation of knowledge and acquisition of academic research tools. These are, therefore, two aims that are not necessarily contradictory, but considering the limited time resources at the college's disposal there is a potential for tension and conflict.

The Waldorf education approach sees the value in academic training and familiarity with the world of education and its concepts, but it does not view them as skills and values that can enrich teaching itself. Steiner, a scientist by training who had the utmost respect for scientific tools and the scientific approach, said on several occasions that a teacher's training in a Waldorf school should not be based on scientific concepts, but on art, humanistic values, study of spiritual writings, and observation of children (Steiner, 1983, Lecture 4).

Consequently, there is tension between the two approaches, and it is manifested when the college administration and heads of the Waldorf program discuss the syllabus and the different emphases of the training. This tension also exists among the students. They can disparage academic knowledge and a scientific approach on the one hand, or view the Waldorf approach as something spiritual and lacking substance on the other.

This tension may also be created among the lecturers of the two approaches. From the perspective of several years' experience it seems to me that understanding and discourse, particularly between the lecturers, and a situation whereby one side respects and recognizes the other's approach can facilitate a connection between the two disciplines among the students, and the motivation and respect they bring to their various classes.

The students' subject training in their chosen field of knowledge may also lead to misunderstanding. In teacher education colleges in Israel, students usually study toward teaching a specific age (kindergarten, elementary school, junior high school, or high school), and at the same time specialize in their discipline of choice—mathematics, nature and science, literature, Bible, and so forth. Almost one-third of all teacher education hours are devoted to this specialization and the practical experience associated with it.

Teacher training in the spirit of Waldorf education emphasizes general humanistic as well as artistic and developmental training, with no specialization in a specific field of knowledge. The premise underlying this approach is that the teachers themselves can supplement the fields of knowledge in elementary school teaching, and that it is more important to invest in general and developmental training (Barz, 2013; Gabert, 1961).

The large number of hours that students in the Waldorf program have to invest in the subject field, at the expense of hours they could utilize for more general and Waldorf-oriented studies, can create tension and difficulties in the connection between the two types of training. It can also engender discord, and the students may lack motivation to engage in the required subject as it does not correspond with Waldorf studies and is often taught differently in Waldorf schools.

Here, too, teachers can exert considerable influence on their students, and much depends on the significance they attribute to the acquisition of subject teaching for future teachers in Waldorf schools, regardless of the teaching method.

The emphasis on the various fields of art can also be a source of misunderstanding and disagreement. The college allows the training program in the spirit of Waldorf education to devote about one-third of teaching hours to the various artistic fields. This poses challenges on several levels: first, the college has to employ lecturers (artists) who have undergone art training in the spirit of Waldorf education, which is sometimes essentially different from conventional art training (Howard, 1998).

Second, a schedule and priorities have to be implemented that are completely different from those of the college. Unlike students in another college program, Waldorf students take a smaller number of theoretical courses in order to allow for art studies that are both broad and in depth. Finally, in some of the arts (such as eurythmy, music, and painting), the students can work in only relatively small groups, and this means additional resources.

On this point I do not see tension or a special challenge to students in the Waldorf program since art studies in addition to the other fields of knowledge "ventilate" the school day and are well liked by the vast majority of students. The challenge lies in convincing the college administration that allows students to take art studies instead of many theoretical courses.

Another bone of contention between the two approaches is student evaluation. Standard evaluation in academic studies is numerical—exams or papers are graded, having tested a specific combination of processed previous knowledge, knowledge gathering, and creative and academic writing ability.

Although the accepted evaluation in Waldorf education can include examinations and papers, it is directed far more to dialogue, discourse, artistic creation in a range of media (which are very difficult to express numerically), and to the teamwork of a number of students on a specific project (Barz, 2013: Gabert, 1961).

Additionally, the evaluation agent is not necessarily the lecturer, and the aspiration is for the students to evaluate themselves and receive feedback and assistance on self-evaluation processes from their colleagues and teachers. Whereas a large part of this alternative evaluation is the routine in the Waldorf training program at the college, an additional, numerical grade must still be given for each course.

The dry, defined numerical grade often constitutes a source of frustration and disappointment for the students. They expect the lecturers in the Waldorf fields (particularly in the arts) to give them a personal, individual, and qualitative evaluation. They are unable to connect the numerical grade with Waldorf learning methods. Frustration sometimes characterizes the lecturers' work, too, as it is difficult for them to evaluate artistic quality, and dialogical work with exact numbers.

Over the years one solution that has been found is an additional evaluation in the spirit of Waldorf education and in the form of a written certificate given to the students (and on occasion to the lecturers by the students) at the end of each year. In this regard the Waldorf program compromises with the accepted form of evaluation and is compelled to accept numerical grades as a final expression of evaluation. This is not an easy compromise and it runs counter to the mind-set and conscience of lecturers and students alike.

CONCLUSION

I have reviewed the teacher training program in the spirit of Waldorf education that is incorporated into David Yellin College of Education in Jerusalem. We began by listing the main principles and characteristics of Waldorf education, as a means to understanding this special form of teacher training. We also discussed admission to the program, monitoring students in the course of their training, student evaluation, and complex relations between teacher training for a Waldorf school and academic studies.

The review clearly shows the potential and advantages of this sort of combined training—Waldorf and academic—and also its possible shortfalls and disadvantages. The advantages lie in the possibility of optimally combining the qualities and opportunities that academic study can provide coupled with the inherent qualities of Waldorf education.

As we have seen, each type of training has a different orientation, and the combination and balance between their qualities can offer students the best of both worlds. For example, this is the only Waldorf education training program in Israel in which the students receive methodic and in-depth teaching in a specific field of knowledge (the sciences, Jewish history, mathematics, language, or literature) in addition to general education studies.

The training program provides the lecturers with a proper place of work and all the accepted social benefits for teachers. Additionally, the training program provides a certificate for work in Waldorf schools as well as a B.Ed. and a teaching certificate, which enables work in any state school in Israel.

The disadvantages are also associated with the combination of the two approaches. First is the danger that studies in each approach—academic on the one hand and Waldorf education on the other—will not be sufficiently in depth due to an attempt to work according to the two approaches.

In the end, Lior could have chosen to study in a private Waldorf training program and then she would have studied only the Waldorf approach, perhaps with a larger number of hours, and more importantly, she could have perhaps devoted more time to the arts or anthroposophical studies.

However, she also could have chosen a regular teacher training program without Waldorf education studies, and then she would almost certainly have delved deeper into academic research. The second danger is that it is difficult to combine the two approaches and in the course of training, Lior—or anyone choosing this track—will have to search within herself and find the ability to do so. After all, they are two ideologically different approaches and it is not easy to combine them into a whole inner training process.

Both the advantages and the disadvantages are linked to combining and integrating two approaches—they can be mutually enriching and reinforce each other's capabilities and qualities, but they can also weaken one another and lead to superficial and deficient learning of both approaches. Consequently, the question facing a training program of this kind is how to reinforce, enrich, and enhance the two different approaches and qualities: academic knowledge abilities on the one hand, and the qualities of Waldorf education and all it implies, on the other.

My experience shows that the key lies in the discourse that takes place between the college administration and its representatives and the heads of the Waldorf program, and the teachers in both approaches. When this discourse is open, sincere, and conducted with goodwill and a willingness to listen and for joint creativity, the students gain the advantages of both approaches. But when the discourse is undermined and gives rise to questions of trust, suspicion, and seclusion, there is a danger that both approaches will be weakened and the students will undergo only partial and deficient training in both.

NOTES

1. For information on Waldorf education institutions in Israel, see www. waldorf.co.il.

2. A combined M.Ed. program with the University of Donau—http://www. kulturnundpaedogogik.at.

REFERENCES

Aloni, N. (2007). *Enhancing humanity: The philosophical foundations of humanistic educa-tion.* London, England: Kluwer Academic Publishers.
Barz, H. (Ed.). (2013). *Unterrichten an Waldorfschulen: Berufsbild Waldorflehrer; Neue Perspektiven zu Praxis, Forschung, Ausbildung.* Part C. Wiesbaden, Germany: Springer.
Bortoft, H. (1996). *The wholeness of nature: Goethe's way toward a science of conscious participation in nature.* London, England: Lindisfarne Press.
Campbell, J. (2008). *The hero with a thousand faces.* Novato, CA: New World Library.
Dietrich, E. (2006). *Die erste Waldorfschule Stuttgart Uhlandshöhe 1919 bis 2004—Daten, Dokumente, Bilder.* Stuttgart, Germany: Freies Geistesleben.
Easton, F. (1997). Educating the whole child "head, heart and hands": Learning from the Waldorf experience. *Theory into Practice, 36,* 87–95.
Edmunds, F. (2004). *Introduction to Steiner education: The Waldorf school.* London, Eng-land: Rudolf Steiner Press.
Eisner, E. W. (2002). What can education learn from the arts about the practice of educa-tion? *The Encyclopedia of Informal Education.* http://www.infed.org/biblio/eisner_arts_and_the_practice_of_education.htm

Gabert, E. (1961). *Lehrerbildung im Sinne der Paedagogik Rudolf Steiners*. Stuttgart, Germany: Verlag Freies Geistesleben.

Howard, M. (1998). *Art as spiritual activity: Rudolf Steiner's contribution to the visual arts*. New York, NY: Anthroposophic Press.

Krishnamurti, J. (1987). *Education and the significance of life. Conversation 51*. http://www.jkrishnamurti.org/krishnamurti-teachings/view-text.php?tid=51&chid=67048&w=&

Leber, S. (1991). *Die Sozialgestalt der Waldorfschule*. Stuttgart, Germany: Freies Geistesleben.

Lievegoed, B. (2003). *Phases: The spiritual rhythms of adult life*. Forest Row, England: Rudolf Steiner Press.

Rawson, M. (2010). Sustainable teacher learning in Waldorf education: A socio-cultural perspective. *RoSE, 1*(2), 26–42.

Richter, T. (Ed.). (2006). *Paedagogischer Auftrag und Unterrichtsziele—vom Lehrplan der Waldorfschule* . Stuttgart, Germany: Freies Geistesleben.

Steiner, R. (1947). *Knowledge of the higher worlds and its attainment*. London, England: Rudolf Steiner Press.

Steiner, R. (1964). *The philosophy of freedom*. London, England: Rudolf Steiner Press.

Steiner, R. (1965). *The education of the child in the light of anthroposophy*. New York, NY: Anthroposophic Press.

Steiner, R. (1972). *An outline of occult science*. New York, NY: Anthroposophic Press.

Steiner, R. (1977). *Die Erneuerung der Paedagogisch-Didaktisch Kunst durch Geisteswissenschaft*. Dornach, Switzerland: Rudolf Steiner Verlag.

Steiner, R. (1978). *Menschenerkenntnis und Unterrichtsgestaltung* . Dornach, Switzerland: Rudolf Steiner Verlag.

Steiner, R. (1980). *Allgemeine Menschenkunde als Grundlage der Paedagogik*. Dornach, Switzerland: Rudolf Steiner Verlag.

Steiner, R. (1983). *Die Paedagogische Grundlage und Zielsetzung der Waldorfschule*. Dornach, Switzerland: Rudolf Steiner Verlag.

Steiner, R. (1984). *An Introduction to eurythmy*. New York, NY: Steiner Books.

Steiner, R. (2008). *Theosophy: An introduction to the supersensible knowledge of the world and the destination of man*. New York, NY: Steiner Books.

Steiner, R. (2010). *Der Paedagogische Wert der Menschenerkenntnis und der Kulturwert der Paedagogik*. Dornach, Switzerland: Rudolf Steiner Verlag.

Volker, F. (2012). *Waldorfpädagogik in der Erziehungswissenschaft: Ein Überblick*. Weinheim, Germany: Beltz Juventa.

Wiechert, C. (2012). *Du sollst sein Rätsel lösen*. Dornach, Switzerland: Verlag am Geothanum.

Zander, H. (2007). *Anthroposophie in Deutschland*. Goettingen, Germany: Vandenhoek & Ruprecht.

UNDERMINING TEACHER EDUCATION

Critic of the Neoliberal Worldview

Shlomo Back

In the neoliberal regime, a new ideal type of person, the "indebted man," emerges (Lazzarato, 2012). His subjectivity is formed within the logic of competition; he is a calculating, instrumentally driven "enterprise man" (Ball, 2013, p. 132). Being an "entrepreneur of himself" (Foucault, 2008, p. 226), he feels free, but "his actions, his behavior, are confined to the limits defined by the debt he has entered into" (Lazzarato, 2012, p. 31). "Deprived as he or she is of the ability to govern his or her time, or to evaluate his or her own behaviors, his or her capacity for autonomous action is strictly curtailed" (Žižek, 2014, p. 44).

In this chapter, I examine the claim that in countries under neoliberal domination, like the United States, teacher education programs are required to operate like an indebted man. While adapting themselves to this modus operandi, the programs are in danger of losing their professional integrity.

FROM *HOMO ECONOMICUS* TO THE INDEBTED MAN

The indebted man is a current incarnation of *homo economicus* (Lazzarato, 2012, p. 31). Following J. S. Mill (1874/2000, p. 101), *homo economicus* is a free individual who does his best to attain happiness. He finds himself in a constant struggle to survive and sustain his well-being in a permanent state of scarce resources. *Homo economicus* is a rational agent. He believes that the "effort-reward" pair is a key to his success. His rationality is technical or instrumental (Weber, 1947).

Although it is clear that human beings are not rational in this sense (Kahneman, Slovic, & Tversky, 1982), classical economic theorists usually assume that the agent's rationality is factually true and normatively appealing (Hahn & Hollis, 1979, pp. 12–13). It is factually true, in the sense that this idealization provides the best possible explanation of how humans actually behave. It is normatively appealing because it suggests how humans should behave if they want to maximize their utility.

From the ethical point of view, Ayn Rand faithfully presents the *homo economicus* ideal:

> Man—every man—is an end in himself, not the means to the ends of others. He must exist for his own sake, neither sacrificing himself to others nor sacrificing others to himself. The pursuit of his own rational self-interest and of his own happiness is the highest moral purpose of his life. The ideal political-economic system is laissez-faire capitalism. It is a system where men deal with one another, not as victims and executioners, nor as masters and slaves, but as traders, by free, voluntary exchange to mutual benefit. (Rand, 1962)

The ideal of *homo economicus* is debated. Instrumental rationality does not always lead to utility maximization. In a completely laissez-faire economy based on free competition in which each individual is rational, his situation is worse than it would be in some kind of cooperative arrangement (Rapoport & Chammah, 1965). Being rational is not always reasonable (Gewirth, 1983). Many thinkers find the ideal of freedom, which legitimizes the *homo economicus*, illusionary (see Back, 2012, for a discussion of this criticism).

These objections notwithstanding, the neoliberal ideology follows the liberal one, and also advances a concept of *homo economicus*, but with a different emphasis. This modified type of *homo economicus* is the "indebted man." In the neoliberal economy, debt becomes a political relation of subjection and enslavement. It is an economy that forces the agents to become indebted.

The creditor-debtor relation is based upon asymmetry of power and not on that of a commercial symmetrical exchange. The behavior of the indebted man is directed toward pleasing his debtor. He is grateful and fears the consequences of not being able to return the debt (Žižek, 2014, p. 44). The indebted man is always in a defensive mood. He has to constantly demonstrate his ability to pay his debts. He is guilty unless proven innocent.

The indebted man is an entrepreneur. He internalizes the "grow or die" imperative (Klein, 2014, p. 21). Supplemented with a demand to consume and upgrade, he is in permanent debt. The indebted man must always invest because what was once a right (e.g., food, shelter, education, health) becomes a personal investment, in which the agent alone is responsible for his own future. If he errs in his investment, he has to pay the price. To protect himself from the possible risky outcomes of his adventures, his decisions are based on "actuarial rationality" (Besley & Peters, 2007, p. 156). He invests in insurance policies and buys the protection that hitherto was given to him by the public services of the welfare state.

The indebted man is in a steady state of competition. Since everyone is an entrepreneur and the resources are limited, he has to demonstrate his superiority over all his rivals. The indebted man cannot be trusted, for to win the competition, he is always seduced to utilize all possible means to maximize his own utility (Mansouri & Rowney, 2014). Hence the necessity of having strict regulations. At the same time, the indebted man is constantly under external evaluation, which activates a punitive accountability system to ensure that he is still able to pay his debts, while keeping all the regulations.

The indebted man is "working on his self" in the sense that "being in debt" is for him a normal situation. But like the Christian original sin, he has to devote his life to return his debts. On the one hand, he is grateful for the opportunity to be in debt. On the other, he feels guilty for the very need to be in debt (Lazzarato, 2012, pp. 7–8). While the utilitarian agenda of *homo economicus* is seen as a way to attain human happiness, being an indebted man distances him from this ideal.

THE NEW ACCOUNTABILITY SYSTEM

Teacher education programs are becoming "indebted," as can be seen from the new discourse about the "accountability system." In recent years, a new kind of teacher education discourse has emerged in the United States. This discourse is visible in new accreditation standards and federal guidelines for assessing programs.[1] These standards require preparation programs to be accountable for outcome-based measures such as graduates' achievements in raising their pupils' test scores.

There is a basic difference between a quality assurance system based on the classical *homo economicus* ideal and an accountability system based on the "indebted man." It is one thing to have a feedback mechanism that encourages professional reflection about how preparation programs function and whether they are reaching their intended goals. It is another to have an accountability system that demonstrates a program's inadequacy.

Having an evaluation system that aims to "provide useful information for the improvement of teacher preparation policy and practice" (Feuer, Floden, Chudowsky, & Ahn, 2013, p. 4) is reasonable. Having an accountability system that ranks preparation programs by levels and determines funding on that basis is not. The first system reflects a culture of trust, the second, a culture of suspicion (O'Neil, 2002). The first encourages self-criticism and learning from successes and failures; the second breeds defensiveness, tension, and anxiety, typical of the indebted man. I argue that the accountability system of teacher education programs, especially since 2009, originates from a culture of suspicion.

THE NEOLIBERAL ARGUMENT FOR A SYSTEM OF ACCOUNTABILITY

The neoliberal case for a teacher education "system of accountability" is quite simple. It fits the general neoliberal charge against public services. Because these services spend public funds, the public has the right to know if its money is appropriately and efficiently used. There is an additional, not-so-hidden agenda to this policy, for the neoliberal regime attempts to abolish the public sector and to transmit all civic services to for-profit organizations (Harvey, 2005). Toward this end, the neoliberal government itself raises the suspicion that public services are inefficient and corrupt.

Budget cuts provide a first step in the implementation of this policy. Under the slogan of "efficiency," the government cuts the budget of public services until they cannot properly function. Then, it can easily validate the claim that the (deprived) services malfunction because they cannot deliver the required goods (Klein, 2007). This claim is supported by establishing an accountability system that provides the evidence for the poor functioning of the deprived public service. Thereafter, the door is open to invite the private sector to be charitable and rescue the services (Saltman, 2008, p. 187).[2]

Beside the general suspicious attitude toward any public service, the argument against teacher education programs contains three specific premises that at first glance seem to be ideologically neutral:

1. The quality of instruction plays a central role in student learning.
2. Teacher preparation programs contribute to the quality of instruction.
3. The evaluation of teacher preparation programs can provide useful information for the improvement of teacher preparation policy and practice. (Feuer et al., 2013, p. 4)

Interpreted from a culture of suspicion, the argument looks quite different. To the first statement of the argument it is essential to add the "how do you decide?" issue, and state as a corollary (which is not in accordance with Feuer et al.) that the quality of instruction is determined by students' achievements on standardized tests. According to this criterion, the quality of the U.S. educational system is mediocre at best and the achievement gaps within the system are enormous because of the bad instruction that the students receive.

The second premise puts the blame on the teachers, since the "quality of the system cannot exceed the quality of its teachers" (McKinsey & Company, 2007). As the McKinsey report emphasizes, "The available evidence suggests that the main driver of the variation in student learning at school is the quality of the teachers" (2007, p. 12). If a system's outcomes are poor, it is because its teachers are not as good as they should be. Such a claim, though undeniably correct, conveys only part of the picture. It underestimates the impact of the many social, economic, and cultural variables on students' learning. It is not fair to blame the teachers alone for the poor achievement of students from low socioeconomic backgrounds.

The argument's third premise is that the teachers are not as good as they should be because they receive inadequate professional preparation. Instead of cultivating expert technicians who prepare students to meet the required standards and pass the exams, too many university-based professional programs produce inept, pseudoprofessionals who replace accountability for achievement with endless discussions about immeasurable "processes."

The teachers they prepare pretend to "educate" pupils. They disguise their inability or reluctance to teach the "basics" by using pedagogical jargon about "empowering" the students, "constructing" knowledge, "building" communities of learners, and enhancing "meaningful" learning. No wonder their pupils achieve poor academic outcomes.

Consequently, preparation programs deserve the suspicious attitude they arouse. The public should not support malfunctioning programs. In order to identify them, we need a reliable and transparent accountability system that will evaluate program quality, assess how programs meet required standards, and publish their grades they earn.

Each of the modified premises is doubtful, if not plainly flawed, a deceptive effort that makes the neoliberal agenda seem reasonable. The corollary to the opening statement, that the quality of the instruction is determined by students' achievements in standardized tests, presents a narrow, one-sided view of the aims of education.

For sure, the quality of the teachers is of utmost importance, and should be evaluated, but teacher quality should not be assessed by inappropriate measurement tools such as their students' scores on standardized achievement tests (Ravitch, 2010). It is simply mistaken (and clearly biased) to move from the children to their teachers and from them to the programs that prepare them. The appeal of the argument is not due to its soundness. Rather, it comes from the populist "look how they are spending/wasting your money" accusation.

FROM QUALITY ASSURANCE TO AN ACCOUNTABILITY SYSTEM

An analysis of the development of the accountability system in the United States strengthens the claim that the system requires preparation programs to move from the *homo economicus* persona to the indebted man. The transformation of accreditation requirements from the National Council for Accreditation of Teacher Education (NCATE) to the Council for the Accreditation of Educator Preparation (CAEP)[3] is instructive. Since the publication of its first accreditation standards in 1957 through 2000, NCATE measured preparation programs according to an "input model" (Lashway, 2001, p. 5). In this model, quality is defined as the program's fitness to/for purposes (Doherty, 2008). A good quality program is judged as being in accord with a certain set of standards.

Each program requesting accreditation prepares a self-review description of what it offers to candidates. The report presents the program's rationale and objectives and demonstrates how the program fulfills them. Programs had to report on six dimensions of their activities: governance; admission and retention of students; faculty teaching, research, and service; curriculum (including the clinical component of the program); evaluation of students; and the context and resources supporting the program (Cruickshank et al., 1991). This process illustrates a strict instrumental rationality, which is supposedly a sign of professionalism and expertise.

After 1957, the conventional wisdom changed. The focus shifted from the teacher to the learner, from teaching to learning, from behaviorism to [social] constructivism, from the view that teaching is an applied science occupation to the understanding of teaching as a profession for reflective practitioners. What is taught, the input, becomes less important than what is learned, the results. Although the results still depend, of course, on what is taught, the idea is to examine whether the input has any impact on the results. So in order to evaluate the program, it is vital to look at its outcomes.[4]

Since 2000, NCATE standards took accountability to an important next step by emphasizing program outcomes. The new standards call for programs to ensure that candidates have acquired the necessary knowledge and skills to become educators and have demonstrated their knowledge and skills in measurable ways. Therefore, they ask: "Has the institution provided clear evidence of the competence of their candidates? Can candidates help students learn?" (NCATE, 2006). To answer these questions, NCATE introduces a "performance-based" set of benchmarks attached to each standard that distinguishes three levels of performance (unacceptable, acceptable, and target).

It is easy to justify the transfer to performance-based indicators of quality. According to the logic of the standards model, if a preparation program functions in a professional manner, its outcome will be competent teachers. Accreditation offers professional assurance that the program knows how to prepare students to be good teachers (though it is up to the program to decide what kind of teacher it prepares (see Christensen, 1996).

But this shift may also be the first step in a move from liberal to neoliberal ideology or from *homo economicus* to the indebted man. For example, the mission of the accreditation system itself acquires a new focus. As seen below, instead of dealing with program quality in terms of input variables, it deals with graduates' achievements measured in terms of student performance on standardized tests.

THE NEW ACCOUNTABILITY SYSTEM

In the 2013 CAEP standards, the focus shifts even further to the accomplishments of the graduates as teachers in schools after they have finished their course of learning. The new accountability system requires program graduates to produce student achievement gains, and the quality of their program depends on this indicator of success. CAEP standards implement the U.S. secretary of education's insistence that the accountability system should "carefully track the performance of teachers in order to identify which programs are producing well-prepared teachers and which programs are not." In this way it will be possible to study and copy "the practices of effective teacher preparation programs—and encourage the lowest-performers to shape up or shut down" (Duncan, 2009).

Duncan's speech illustrates a new kind of discourse in teacher education that promotes the development of an accountability system which seeks:

1. To provide public understanding of the extent to which public and private, "traditional" and "alternative" programs are graduating teachers who have the knowledge and skills necessary to educate each student they teach to the highest learning standards; 2. To undergird appropriate state and federal oversight and accountability, and thus to enable officials to either identify excellence or to impose sanctions when programs fail to demonstrate adequate effectiveness; and 3. To facilitate the continuous improvement of preparation programs by program staff and faculty. (Allen, Coble, & Crow, 2014, p. 4)

The second aim tells the whole story. It is a significant addition to the traditional purposes of the evaluation system—"holding programs accountable for producing well trained and effective educators; providing consumer information to prospective students and their potential future employers, and supporting program self-improvement" (Feuer et al., 2013, p. 4).

At this point quality assurance is transformed into a managerial tool. While administrative decisions should be "data based" or "data informed," everything turns on the parameters used to evaluate the programs. If the standards refer only to the outcomes of the programs and ignore the antecedents as well as the program's functioning, this is not a case of responsive evaluation (Stake, 2001), which aims to help improve the programs by suggesting how the program can become a better one.[5]

The use of the accreditation system to enforce governmental regulations is evident in new regulations of the U.S. Department of Education released in December 2014. The regulations aim to

> implement requirements for the teacher preparation program accountability system . . . that would result in the development and distribution of more meaningful data on teacher preparation program quality. (USDE, 2014)

This means that the main indicator of the quality of the program should be "the aggregate learning outcomes of students taught by new teachers." That is, "the ability of the program's graduates to produce gains in student learning." In addition, the regulations mention other outcomes, such as "placement and retention rates of program graduates and survey data from past graduates and their employers" (USDE, 2014).

The department declares that the improved system, applicable to both traditional and alternative-route programs,

> would enable prospective teachers to make more informed choices about their enrollment in a teacher preparation program and employers of prospective teachers to make more informed hiring decisions. Further, the proposed regulations would also create incentives for States and institutes of higher education to monitor and continuously improve the quality of their teacher preparation programs, informed by more meaningful data. Most importantly, elementary and secondary school students would benefit from these proposed regulations because the feedback loop created would lead to better prepared, higher quality teachers in classrooms, especially for students in high-need schools and communities who are disproportionately taught by newer teachers. (USDE, 2014)

Another aim of the regulations, mentioned only later, has far-reaching financial consequences. Based on program and state reports, preparation programs will be ranked on the basis of four levels with only high-quality teacher preparation programs eligible for federal funding.

The logic of the indebted man is evident here. The government funds are seen as an investment that has to be immediately fruitful. It has definite indicators of success. The preparation programs are debtors that have to demonstrate their ability to produce efficient outcomes (e.g., effective teachers). Behaving like stakeholders in a financial corporation, the authorities demand annual reports of achievements, provide benchmarks for comparison, and enforce a climate of competition. The accountability system is both a power mechanism and an insurance policy. It requires that the program will "work on itself" and will constantly check its ability to pay its debts, and thus guarantee its striving for improvement.

The preparation programs are indebted to the public and to themselves to produce effective teachers. It is a permanent debt, and the "producers" (as they are aptly called) need to assure the stakeholders that they can repay it. The creditor-debtor power relation puts them in a permanent defensive position. They are a priori weak unless they prove their strengths. They have to constantly justify their very existence and fear the consequences of not being able to return their debt. They have to persuade the stakeholders that they are professional and trustworthy. The accreditation system provides them with an external insurance policy. As long as they pay the system's requirements, they will be safe.

The requirement of self-report adds another dimension to this picture. Usually, the institution or program seeking accreditation prepares an in-depth self-evaluation report that measures its performance against the standards established by the accrediting system. One of the new accreditation requirements is that the culture of self-study will be part of the program's DNA. For example, Standard 5 of CAEP (2015) requires that

> the provider maintains a quality assurance system comprised of valid data from multiple measures, including evidence of candidates' and completers' positive impact on P–12 student learning and development. The provider supports continuous improvement that is sustained and evidence-based, and that evaluates the effectiveness of its completers. The provider uses the results of inquiry and data collection to establish priorities, enhance program elements and capacity, and test innovations to improve completers' impact on P–12 student learning and development.

This standard makes self-report an essential part of the program's activities. Like the indebted man, program leaders in a culture of suspicion are inclined to ask "What is wrong with me?" (and not simply "How am I doing?") and internalize a defensive, apologetic attitude (see Atkinson, 2012; Bleakley, 2000; Martin & McLellan, 2007 for empirical support). Even more problematic is the danger that this attitude will permeate the programs. In a culture of competition and suspicion, every self-report of students, faculty, and courses might become a tool of governance, power, and control.

The strong objections to the U.S. Department of Education's 2014 proposal reveal its real intent. The opposition, expressed in letters to the secretary of education, includes university-based teacher educators and alternative-route organizations. Although in these letters the authors agree that having a system of accountability is a good idea, they see the new regulations as "a new cudgel to punish teacher preparation programs" (The Association of Teacher Educators, 2015). They reject the specific requirements of the proposed regulations on several grounds:

Technical difficulties: The proposed regulations are unworkable because there are too many preparation programs (The American Association of Colleges for Teacher Education, 2015).

Financial difficulties: The regulations will be too expensive and will divert limited resources from the programs (The Association of Teacher Educators, 2015).

Efficacy problems: The system widens the institutional work load, with no evidence as to its efficiency or relevance (The American Association of Colleges for Teacher Education, 2015).

Ideological problems: Especially disturbing is the attempt to extend the K–12 "test and punish" model into higher education, by using the value-added methodology to measure teacher effectiveness, a method that is "fragile at best" (The American Association of Colleges for Teacher Education, 2015).

Social problems: Preparation programs that serve high-needs schools may be disadvantaged by these regulations given the regulation's reliance on value-added type measures resulting from standardized testing (The Association of Teacher Educators, 2015).

Also, the regulations would negatively affect affordability and access to college for many students [objection raised by the Association of Teacher Educators] because they would limit access to federal financial assistance for teacher candidates (Teacher Education Assistance for College and Higher Education grants).

These objections do not question the necessity of a reliable accountability system. Most of the letters even accept the idea that program quality could be evaluated by the achievement scores of pupils in graduates' classrooms. But they regard the specific proposal as impracticable and inefficient, and warn that "it will add burdensome data collection and reporting requirements for the purpose of identifying and sanctioning the relatively small percentage of programs that are of lower quality" (The National Association for Alternative Certification, 2015).

Outcome indicators of quality do not eliminate the need to address various input indicators. In their report *Building an Evidence-Based System for Teacher Preparation*, Allen et al. (2014) apologize that their Candidate Selection Profile do[es] not involve measures of candidate or completer performance, and they thus do not in that sense convey candidate or program outcomes. Nonetheless . . . the indicators address key concerns that teacher educators, policymakers, and education leaders have about the strength, diversity, and aptitude for teaching of the candidates who enter and complete teacher preparation programs.

One indicator of candidates' strength is their "teaching promise." This criterion highlights the report's emphasis on measuring something that is unmeasurable. "Teaching promise" refers to "attitudes, values, and behaviors"—"the percent of accepted program candidates whose score on a rigorous and validated 'fitness for teaching' assessment demonstrates a strong promise for teaching." The justification of this indicator is that "preparation programs, school districts, and national organizations like Teach for America and UTeach all seek to measure individual attitudes, values, and behaviors that may predict suitability for and success in teaching" (Allen et al., 2014).

Although the report acknowledges that "there is little research evidence linking specific beliefs, values, or habits to measures of teaching quality or teacher effectiveness," it concludes that

there is reason to believe that programs could make effective use of protocols that seek to determine "goodness of fit" between an applicant seeking admission and the career that she or he hopes to join. (Allen et al., 2014)

If adopted in a spirit of inquiry, the field of teacher education could learn a lot from such efforts to predict who is "fit" for teaching. But the authors of the report themselves mention two difficulties in implementing this indicator. The first is "to envision programs reporting results of their screening of individual candidates or for cohorts of applicants/admitted students in a way that supports easy-to-use comparisons across programs or states." The second "is the need to find one or more 'teaching promise' metrics that can be linked directly to important components of high quality classroom teaching." They believe, however, that these obstacles can and should be overcome (Allen et al., 2014).

The report's remarks disclose a fallacious way of reasoning. Teachers' dispositions are highly important, but the term refers to something unquantifiable. Disposition is a fuzzy term, and "being a good teacher includes some mysterious qualities" (M. Ben-Peretz, personal commu-nication, 2 Oct. 2015). The best methods to learn the candidate's "fit-ness for teaching" is to look at his background and to speak with him about his life experiences and his educational vision. Though these methods do not provide a metric and do not "support comparison across programs or states" (Allen et al., 2014), they do indicate who the candidate "is" as a prospective teacher.

THE IMPACT ON TEACHER EDUCATION

Perhaps the idea of an accountability system that emphasizes output indicators of quality does not go far enough. The Relay Graduate School of Education (RGSE) opened its teacher preparation program in New York City in the fall of 2011. It is an alternative-route program, conducted in a nonacademic environment, which has a license to award student a recognized graduate degree—the master of arts in teaching (MAT). The program does not teach theoretical knowledge in educa-tion. Instead of regular courses, RGSE's curriculum comprises some sixty modules, each focused on a different teaching technique (follow-ing Lemov, 2010).[6] Forty percent of the coursework is online and face-to-face meetings are held in small groups for expanding on any given technique.

RGSE proudly claims that it is "the first ever to require its graduate students to demonstrate proficiency and student achievements while teaching full-time in their K–12 classrooms to earn a MAT degree" (Relay School of Education, 2012). The exit requirements of the pro-gram contain, in addition to "successfully complete the Alternate Cer-tification program and demonstrate proficiency in concrete techniques and strategies," the requirement that program graduates "generate [school] student achievement gains in their classrooms." Thereafter program's students will be eligible to earn their master's degree after a second year of committed effort (Relay School of Education, 2011).

The above quotes, taken from the program's website, demonstrate that RGSE sells itself as being the best available commodity in the market of teacher preparation. RGSE is a "for-profit" enterprise, and it promises to be the "first ever" product to be accountable for the effec-tiveness of its graduates, which makes the program a perfect investment. The program's outcomes are well defined; their quality can be objectively measured. It presupposes that teaching is a commodity that sells "student achievement gains," while the good teacher is just the efficient vendor of that commodity. Clearly, these are unrealizable assertions.

AN ALTERNATIVE ROUTE TO THE ALTERNATIVE ROUTE

In the age of huge databases, powerful search engines, and virtual clouds, it is quite easy to collect information and disseminate it. It is much more challenging to collect appropriate data and use it prudently and for good causes. The requirement to be accountable in a culture of suspicion is far from the idea of quality assurance in times of trust.

Today's accountability systems seem to favor alternative-route programs. If input indicators are less important, the door is open to programs whose very possibility to maintain high-quality standards of input features, such as the curriculum, the faculty, the learning processes or the learning resources, is low. Weakening these requirements, on behalf of immediate outcome indicators, strengthens the alternative-route programs, whose operations might be cheaper and shorter. At the same time, this move weakens the professionalization of teaching and reduces its aims to a simplistic and unidimensional vision. It may also weaken the quality of teaching provided to students in most need of well-prepared teachers.

The really disturbing question is whether preparation programs that earn an "exceptionally good" mark in the output model also educate good teachers. The answer depends on the definition of the "good" teacher, which is an ideological issue (Back, 2012; Feiman-Nemser, 1990; Fenstermacher & Soltis, 2009; Sockett, 2008). Nevertheless, I suspect that a technician who graduates from an "exceptionally good" program like the RGSE will not be able to address the real challenges of twenty-first-century students. High achievements on high-stakes, standardized tests do not necessarily reflect meaningful learning, and while technical reasoning is important, it is limited and does not serve the majority of students in school.

Zygmunt Bauman (2005), a famous sociologist who coined the term the "liquid society," observes that formal education is becoming irrelevant, even destructive to the needs of our next generation. Formal education is, by its very nature, conservative and stable. It aims to preserve and deliver to the new generation well-established ideas, ideals, values, and/or attitudes that seem to have lasting significance. We live in a postmodern (or "liquid") world in which the pace of the change accelerates daily. In our consumerist era, what is new is always better (for constant consuming is a condition to the formation of the indebted man).

If the traditional articles of faith cease to be relevant and cannot survive the day, formal education loses its raison d'être. In the postmodern world, the status of knowledge is debatable, ethically driven principles are doubtful, aesthetic evaluations are highly questionable, and even God is dead. But if one cannot rely anymore on any durable conception of "the good," the "beautiful," the "true," or the "divine," we may question whether education still has something valuable to offer the new generation.

Not surprisingly, the so-called crisis of education is a widespread phenomenon in the Western world. In an age in which the written word is losing its priority to the image, and every stimulus should be as short, dynamic, colorful, and noisy as possible, classroom experiences seem outdated and boring. The price for this anachronism is huge. Schools become more irrelevant than ever to real life and teachers lose their authority and influence on the children's lives.

This educational crisis cannot be addressed by enforcing an even more rigid accountability system. High-stakes outcome measures are neither what students want nor what they deserve. But, teaching, of course, is much more than a profession dedicated to enabling students to pass exams. It is even more than transmitting knowledge to the next generation. It requires devotion to the future of the students and their society. It involves the art of enhancing the students' well-being.

In a romantic flavor, the good teacher is an authentic person who cares for pupils and enhances their creativity, their critical stance, and their capacity for self-fulfillment (Back, 2012). For this to happen, we have to abandon the indebted man model and withdraw from the *homo economicus* way of rational, though not always reasonable, thinking.

Following Aristotle (1984), MacIntyre (2007), and Sennett (2008), I propose that the teacher's goal (*telos*) is intrinsic to his professional activity (e.g., to foster learning), although teaching might have external aims as well. In a viable education process, each student is required to undertake a *Bildung*[7] quest with the goals of developing his or her personal and cultural identity. In this journey, the learner addresses all available knowledge sources (humanities, arts, and sciences) to answer the question "Who am I as a unique person and as a human being?"

To fully investigate this question, the individual should be ready to leave the safe shores of his or her usual habitus and delve into a self-identity quest (Serres, 1997). It is a nomadic process, which can be either physical or virtual, in any imaginable place and time. To be significant, this personal journey should be accompanied by a responsible, professional educator. And such a mission clearly changes the role of the teacher, who becomes a pedagogue in the original sense of the Greek term.[8]

Thus, it is necessary to envisage a very different kind of alternative teacher education program, which will address the real needs of teachers and students in the twenty-first century. Such programs, will not limit itself to ask "what teachers need to know and be able to do" (Darling-Hammond & Bransford, 2005). It will also address the question of *"who the teacher is"* (Palmer, 1998).

These programs will question the moral basis of the society and suggest that solidarity and communality are no less significant than individuality and competition. They will probe whether equality is no less noteworthy than illusionary individual freedom, whether dialogue and tolerance are no less important than efficiency and material success. These programs do not conceive of humans as commodities, and for them, material wealth is not a guarantee of human happiness.

One such program is ACE (Active-Collaborative-Education), a teacher education program for postgraduate students conducted in the Kaye College of Education. In the program the student is requested to wander in an unknown territory (Back & Shachor, 2016). He has no paved roads to follow and no predefined targets to conquer. He becomes a teacher, by understanding the meaning he gives to "teaching," "learning," and "students."

One aspect of ACE is that it has no predefined measurable aims, no benchmarks, and no grades. If the standards of the accountability system would have been applied to ACE, the program would not be ranked as one of the best. Nevertheless, in 2013 the program had been awarded as the best teacher education program in Israel. The number of candidates wishing to study in the program exceeds the number of available places, and the program's graduates are welcomed in the district's kindergartens and schools.

The reason, I believe, is simple: the program deals with the teacher as a human being. It is occupied with self-development and doubts "objective" measurements. It deals with quality and not with standards. And it accepts the view that quality is a qualitative notion,[9] which has to be evaluated in qualitative methods. For sure, this is a subjective evaluation, but the very idea of objectivity hides the questions of who benefits from the objective measurement and who decides about the essence of the indicators. The race after accountability has to be replaced by a quest for genuine quality.

NOTES

I would like to thank Miriam Ben-Peretz, Ariela Gidron, Sharon Feiman-Nemser, and Sarah Shimoni for carefully reading of earlier drafts of this chapter and suggesting many valuable comments.

1. For example: National Council for Accreditation of Teacher Education (NCATE, 2010); Council for the Accreditation of Educator Preparation, (CAEP, 2015); United States Department of Education (USDE, 2014); The National Council on Teacher Quality (Greenberg, J., McKee, A., & Walsh, K., 2015); Allen, Coble, & Crow, 2014.

2. This does not happen in Israel, as far as teacher education is concerned. In general, the Israeli educational system is mainly public, although it is divided according to religious and ethnic sectors of the society.

3. CAEP is a new accreditation agency that incorporates NCATE and TEAC (Teacher Education Accreditation Council).

4. The definition of learning outcomes (LO) established by the Bologna working group on qualifications: "LO are what a learner is expected to know, understand and/or be able to do at the end of a period of learning" (retrieved from http://che.org.il/wp-content/uploads/2012/04/).

5. I am in debt to Prof. Ben-Peretz for reminding me of Stake's theory.

6. For example, Technique 7 (4MS) tells the teachers that it is vital to design effective objectives.

To do so, use the criteria below to determine if your objective is effective:

1. Manageable: An objective can't be effective if you can't teach it in a single lesson. Of course you want your students to master larger skills,

but this can take weeks so you need to break them into steps your students can master in one period.
2. Measureable: Effective objectives can be measured. This is often done at the end of the period with an exit ticket (a short activity or question students complete to show they learned the material).
3. Made first: An objective should guide the activities you use in the lesson and not simply be an afterthought.
4. Most important: Choose an objective based on what is *most* important for students to learn on the path to college. (Lemov, 2010, 60–62)

7. The *Bildung* process mainly concerns human "inner improvement and elevations" as he "seeks to grasp as much world as possible and bind it as tightly as he can to himself" (von Humboldt, 1793/2000, pp. 58–59). As Seigel explains, *Bildung* is "a process . . . in which the singular potential inherent in particular individuals could find realization in the world: life in society helped bring the self to cognizance of its own needs and powers because the persons and conditions it encountered there help to reveal the inner structure of its own being" (2005, p. 333).

8. For a detailed discussion of these ideas, see Back and Shachor (2016).

9. In the past, quality was a primary concept that could not be analyzed or reduced to other concepts (Pirsig, 1974). The recognition that something is (or has) high or good "quality" comes prior to the question of what makes it so. The supposition is that something has high quality if it is extraordinary and unique. Beethoven's Ninth Symphony has high quality, not because there are many like it, but because it is inimitable, because there is something special about it, because it defies any standard. Its holistic *gestalt* renders it unique. The feeling that nothing is missing and nothing can be added makes it perfect. Even if one discovers why it is superb, it is impossible to reproduce something like it. This is a qualitative notion of quality. Such quality is decided by direct meeting. You have to "see" the object in order to perceive its quality. This qualitative notion of quality is based on the idea of a deep encounter between the "good" entity and the one who observes or encounters it.

REFERENCES

Allen, N., Coble, C., & Crowe, E. (2014). *Building an evidence-based system for teacher preparation*. Washington, DC: Teacher Preparation Analytics (TPA).
The American Association of Colleges for Teacher Education. (2015). *Concerns with the U.S. Department of Education's Proposed Regulations for Teacher Preparation Programs*. Retrieved on February 2, 2015 from https://secure.aacte.org/apps/rl/res_get.php?fid=1588&ref=res.

Aristotle. (1984). Nicomachean ethics (W. Ross, Trans. & revised by J. Urmson, Trans.). In J. Barnes (Ed.). *The complete works of Aristotle* (Revised Oxford Translation ed., Vol. 2, pp. 1729–1867). Princeton, NJ: Princeton University Press.

The Association of Teacher Educators. (2015). *Letter to U.S. Department of Education.* Retrieved on February 2, 2015 from http://www.ate1.org/uploads/file/ATEcommentson-teacherprepregs.pdf.

Atkinson, B. M. (2012). Strategic compliance silence, "faking it," and confession in teacher reflection. *Journal of Curriculum Theorizing, 28*(1), 74–87.

Back, S. (2012). *Ways of learning to teach.* Rotterdam, Netherlands: Sense.

Back, S., & Shachor, R. M. 2016. The "third" within ACE. In J. Barak & A. Gidron (Eds.), *Active collaborative education: A journey towards teaching* (pp. 149–167). Rotterdam, Netherlands: Sense.

Ball, S. J. (2013). *Foucault, power, and education.* New York, NY: Routledge.

Bauman, Z. (2005). Education in liquid modernity. *Review of education, pedagogy, and cultural studies, 27*(4), 303–317.

Besley, T. A., & Peters, M. A. (2007). *Subjectivity & truth: Foucault, education, and the culture of self.* New York, NY: Peter Lang.

Bleakley, A. (2000). Adrift without a life belt: Reflective self-assessment in a post-modern age. *Teaching in Higher Education, 5*(4), 405–418. doi:10.1080/713699179

CAEP (Council for the Accreditation of Educator Preparation). (2015). *CAEP Accreditation Standards (2013).*

Christensen, D. (1996). The professional knowledge-research base for teacher education. In J. Sikula (Ed.), *Handbook of research on teacher education* (2nd ed., pp. 38–52). New York, NY: Macmillan.

Cruickshank, D. R., McCullough, J. D., Reynolds, R. T., Troyer, M. B., & Crux, J. J. (1991). *The legacy of NCATE: An analysis of standards and criteria for compliance since 1957* (ERIC document no. 339686).

Darling-Hammond, L., & Bransford, J. (Eds.). (2005). *Preparing teachers for a changing world.* San Francisco, CA: Jossey-Bass.

Doherty, G. D. (2008). On quality in education. *Quality Assurance in Education, 16*(3), 255–265.

Duncan, A. (2009). *Policy address on teacher preparation.* Retrieved on February 16, 2017 from http://www.tc.columbia.edu/articles/2009/october/arne-duncan-full-transcript.

Feiman-Nemser, S. (1990). Teacher Preparation: Structural and Conceptual Alternatives. In W. R. Houston (Ed.), *Handbook of Research on Teacher Education* (pp. 212–233). NY: McMillan Publishing Company.

Fenstermacher, G., Soltis, J. F. (2009). *Approaches to Teaching* (5th ed.). NY: Teachers College Press.

Feuer, M. J., Floden, R. E., Chudowsky, N., & Ahn, J. (2013). *Evaluation of teacher preparation programs.* Washington, DC: National Academy of Education.

Foucault, M. (2008). *The birth of biopolitics* (G. Burchell, Trans.). New York, NY: Palgrave Macmillan.

Gewirth, A. (1983). The rationality of reasonableness. *Synthese, 57*(225), 248.

Greenberg, J., McKee, A., & Walsh, K. (2015). *2014 teacher preparation review: A review of the nation's teacher education programs.* Washington, DC: National Council on Teacher Quality (NCTQ).

Hahn, F., & Hollis, M. (Eds.). (1979). *Philosophy and economic theory.* Oxford, England: Oxford University Press.

Harvey, D. (2005). *A brief history of neoliberalism.* New York, NY: Oxford University Press.

Kahneman, D., Slovic, P., & Tversky, A. (Eds.). (1982). *Judgement under uncertainty: Heuristics and biases.* Cambridge, England: Cambridge University Press.

Klein, N. (2007). *The shock doctrine: The rise of disaster capitalism.* New York, NY: Henry Holt.

Klein, N. (2014). *This changes everything.* London, England: Allen Lane.

Lashway, L. (2001). *The new standards and accountability.* Eugene, OR: Eric Clearinghouse on Educational Management. College of Education, University of Oregon.

Lazzarato, M. (2012). *The making of the indebted man* (J. D. Jordan, Trans.). Cambridge, MA: MIT Press.

Lemov, D. (2010). *Teach Like a Champion: 49 Techniques that put students on the path to college.* San Francisco: Jossey-Bass.

MacIntyre. (2007). *After virtue* (3rd ed.). Notre Dame, IN: University of Notre Dame Press.

Mansouri, M., & Rowney, J. (2014). The dilemma of accountability for professionals: A challenge for mainstream management theories. *Journal of Business Ethics, 123,* 5–56.

Martin, J., & McLellan, A.-M. (2007). The educational psychology of self-regulation: A conceptual and critical analysis. *Studies in Philosophy and Education, 27*(6), 433–448. doi:10.1007/s11217-007-9060-4

McKinsey & Company. (2007). *How the best-performing school systems come out on top.* McKinsey & Company. http://mckinseyonsociety.com/how-the-worlds-best-performing-schools-come-out-on-top/

Mill, J. S. (1874/2000). *Essays on some unsettled questions of political economy* (2nd ed.). London, England: Batoche Books.

The National Association for Alternative Certification. (2015). *Response to teacher preparation regulations.* Retrieved on February 2, 2015 from http://www.alternativecertification.org/wp-content/uploads/2015/11/NAAC-response-to-teacher-prep-regulations.pdf.

NCATE (National Council for Accreditation of Teacher Education). (2002). *Professional Standards for the Accreditation of Schools, Colleges, and Departments of Education.* www.ncate.org.

NCATE (National Council for Accreditation of Teacher Education). (2006). *Professional Standards for the Accreditation of Schools, Colleges, and Departments of Education.* http://www.ncate.org/documents/standards/unit_stnds_2006.pdf.

NCATE (National Council for Accreditation of Teacher Education). (2010). *Transforming teacher education through clinical practice: A national strategy to repair effective teachers.* Washington, DC: National Council for Accreditation of Teacher Education.

O'Neil, O. (2002). *Called to Account.* Retrieved from http://www.bbc.co.uk/radio4/reith2002/

Palmer, P. (1998). *The courage to teach.* San Francisco: Jossey-Bass.

Pirsig, R. M. (1974). *Zen and the art of motorcycle maintenance.* New York, NY: Bantam Books.

Rand, A. (1962). *Objectivism on one foot.* Retrieved August 20, 2008, from http://aynrandlexicon.com

Rapoport, A., & Chammah, A. (1965). *The prisoner's dilemma: A study of conflict and cooperation.* Ann Arbor: University of Michigan Press.

Ravitch, D. (2010). *The death and life of the great American school system: How testing and choice are undermining education.* New York, NY: Basic Books.

Relay School of Education. (2011). *In February, 2011.* Retrieved on February 16, 2017 from http://web.archive.org/web/20110410174340/http://www.relayschool.org/.

Relay School of Education. (2012). *Relay Graduate School of Education.* Retrieved on February 16, 2017 from https://specialevents.cce.columbia.edu/spring-career-fair-2012/relay-graduate-school-education.

Saltman, K., J. (2008). Schooling in disaster capitalism. In D. Boyles (Ed.), *The corporate assault on youth* (pp. 187–218). New York, NY: Peter Lang.

Seigel, J. (2005). *The idea of the self.* Cambridge, England: Cambridge University Press.

Sennett, R. (2008). *The craftsman.* London, England: Allen Lane.

Serres, M. (1997). *The troubadour of knowledge* (F. Faria Glaser, Trans.). Ann Arbor: University of Michigan Press.

Sockett, H. (2008). The moral and epistemic purposes of teacher education. In M. Cochran-Smith, S. Feiman-Nemser, & D. McIntyre (Eds.), *Handbook of research on teacher education* (3rd ed., pp. 45–65). NY: Routledge/Taylor & Francis Group; The Association of Teacher Educators.

Stake, R. E. (2001). Program evaluation, particularly responsive evaluation. In G. F. Madaus, M. Scriven, & D. L. Stufflebeam (Eds.), *Evaluation models: Viewpoints on educational and social services evaluation* (pp. 287–310). Boston, MA: Kluwer.

USDE (U.S. Department of Education). (2014). *Federal Register: Teacher Preparation Issues*, 79 Cong. Rec. 71820.

von Humboldt, W. (1793/2000). Theory of Bildung (G. Horton-Kruger, Trans.). In I. Westbury, S. Hopmann, & K. Riquarts (Eds.), *Teaching as a reflective practice: The German Didaktik tradition* (pp. 57–61). Mahwah, NJ: Erlbaum.

Weber, M. (1947). *The theory of social and economic organizations* (A. Henderson & T. Parsons, Trans.). London, England: Free Press of Glencoe.

Žižek, S. (2014). *Trouble in paradise*. London, England: Allen Lane.

INDEX

ABOUT THE EDITORS AND CONTRIBUTORS

EDITORS

Miriam Ben-Peretz is professor emerita at the Faculty of Education at the University of Haifa where she served as chair of the Department of Teacher Education and dean of the School of Education. She was also president of Tel-Hai College. Her main research and writing interests are curriculum, teacher education and professional development, policy making, and Jewish education. Among her publications are *Learning from Experience: Memory and the Teacher's Account of Teaching* (1995), *Policy-Making in Education: A Holistic Approach in Response to Global Changes* (Rowman & Littlefield, 2009), and *Teacher Educators as Members of an Evolving Profession* (Rowman & Littlefield, 2012). A member of the American National Academy of Education, Prof. Ben-Peretz received AERA's Lifetime Achievement Award (Division C) and Legacy Award (Division K). She was the 2006 laureate of the Israel Prize for Research in Education and in 2015, she received the Israeli prime minister's award, the EMET Prize, for her contribution to educational research.

Sharon Feiman-Nemser is the Jack, Joseph and Morton Mandel Professor of Jewish Education at Brandeis University where she founded the Mandel Center for Studies in Jewish Education and the master of arts in teaching (MAT) program. She also served on the education faculties at the University of Chicago and Michigan State University. A pioneer in research on teacher learning, she has written extensively on teacher education, learning to teach, mentoring, and new teacher induction. *Teachers as Learners*, a collection of her seminal writings, was published in 2012. She was the first recipient of the Margaret Lindsey Award for Outstanding Research from the American Association of Colleges of Teacher Education (1996).

EDITORIAL BOARD

Dr. **Ariela Gidron** is an academic editor of the MOFET Publication House and retired teacher educator in the ACE program at Kaye Academic College of Education. Her research interests include academic writing, narrative approaches to teacher education, and the study of life stories.

Sarah Shimoni is a senior lecturer in the Israeli teacher education system. She currently serves as an academic editor in the MOFET Publication House. Her latest publications relate to teacher educators' discourses and the grounded theory approach in qualitative research.

CONTRIBUTORS

Jacqueline Cossentino is the director of research at the National Center for Montessori in the Public Sector. Since 1999, her research has focused on the development of teaching expertise within the culture of Montessori education. Her work on the subject appears in the *American Journal of Education*, *Curriculum Inquiry*, and the *Journal of Teacher Education*.

Carolyn Pope Edwards, Ed.D., is Cather Professor Emeritus at the University of Nebraska, Lincoln, with joint appointments in the Departments of Psychology and Child, Youth, and Family Studies. She received her doctoral degree in human development from Harvard University and has taught at the Universities of Massachusetts, Kentucky, and Nebraska. Much of her writing describes the innovative public early childhood services of Reggio Emilia and Pistoia, Italy, famous for fostering "one hundred languages" of children; beautiful spaces and design; strong home-school partnerships; and sustained inclusion of all children.

Lella Gandini is the U.S. liaison for the dissemination of the Reggio Emilia approach and the associate editor of the journal *Innovation in Early Childhood Education: The International Reggio Exchange*. A visiting scholar at Lesley University, she has held faculty positions at the University of Massachusetts and Smith College. Gandini's numerous books for educators and parents include *The Hundred Languages of Children: The Reggio Emilia Approach to Early Childhood Education* and *In the Spirit of the Studio: Learning from the Atelier of Reggio Emilia*, 1st and 2nd ed.

Gilad Goldshmidt cofounded Kibbutz Harduf and the first Waldorf School in Israel, where he is still teaching. Gilad is teaching in David Yellin Academic College in Jerusalem, Tel-Hai Academic College and Oranim Academic College specializing in Waldorf education, alternative education, and spirituality in education.

Dafna Granit-Dgani is the director of the southern district of the Institute for Democratic Education, head of the Shvilim academic program, pedagogical counselor, and group facilitator. She was the principal of an alternative school that specialized in project-based learning (PBL) and social activism. Married with three children, she lives in Moshav "Sde Zvi" in the north of the Negev.

Dr. **Raviv Reichert** teaches courses of democratic education and practices as pedagogical mentor in two democratic teacher's training programs: the Shvilim Program at Kaye College and the Hamama Program in Seminar Hakibbutzim College. He also instructs seminars on democratic education in the master's degree of democratic education program at Tel Aviv University, and teaches at the Democratic School in Hadera. He lives in Zoran with his wife and two sons.

Esther Yogev has majored in American history and in the history of education. Yogev lectured at the Kibbutzim College of Education and at the History Departments of Tel-Aviv University. At present, Prof. Yogev serves as the provost of the Kibbutzim College of Education and conducts research on the dilemmas facing history education in regions beset by unresolved ethno-political conflicts. In addition to various articles on her subjects, Prof. Yogev has published two books (in Hebrew): *Histories: Towards a Dialogue with the Israeli Past* with E. Naveh (2002) and *General Knowledge and Culture Infrastructure: Challenges and Objectives in Teacher Training and Higher Education* with N. Aloni, I. Avisar, and D. Hopp (2008).

Shlomo Back is a professor of Philosophy of Education at Kaye Academic College of Education. He served as the college president, and currently he is the head of the M.Teach program. His books include: *Ways of Learning to Teach* (Sense, 2012), *The Technical Vision: The Case of Teacher Education* (2005, Hebrew), and he edited the book *Information, Knowledge and Cognizance: The DNA of Education* (2016, Hebrew).